THE MIND AC·CEL'ER·A'TOR V.1 / MIND' AKSEL'ERAT'ER/ **1** ENGINEERED METHODOLOGIES OF MIND CONDITIONING THAT WILL REINVENT YOUR VERY IDENTITY **2** A COMPENDIUM OF STRATEGY PROVEN TO BOOST THE POWER OF YOUR INTELLECT AND IGNITE THE DORMANT REGIONS OF YOUR BRAIN **3** SYSTEMS OF MENTAL ACUITY THAT WILL INTENSIFY YOUR ABILITY TO LEARN AND ABSORB INFORMATION **4** A PROGRAM THAT WILL FORGE THE USER A FUTURE AND LAUNCH THE USER TOWARDS THAT FUTURE.

THE MIND ACCELERATOR
IS YOUR LEXICON FOR SUCCESS

The first release from the team at Volition Thought House, *The Mind Accelerator* is not a collection of general philosophies, nor is it your mainstream self-help book of the week. This is a manual for the profession of achievement, a refinement of centuries of theory and thought, and an innovation of groundbreaking proportions. This manual draws upon a progression of research from that of Bulgarian educational psychiatrist Dr. Georgi Lozanov and mind development pioneer Dr. Win Wenger, to Noble Laureates such as neuroscientist Roger Sperry and neurobiologist Gerald Edelman. It takes into account the genius of physicist Albert Einstein, the revelations of Roman Emperor Marcus Aurelius, the theoretical propositions of Socrates, and the literary mystery of James Allen.

The Mind Accel  ll walks of
life: Ivy League teenagers,

Generation X business magnates and hot dog vendors, buyers and sellers, housewives and political leaders, programmers and hackers, inlaws and outlaws, thinkers and labourers, priests and lawyers, shoe makers and stock brokers. No matter what your persuasion, this industrial-strength tool will redefine your identity, power you to think and process information at a god-like level, absorb information at the speed of *sight*, evolve your capabilities to that of a divine being, and launch your life in an upward ascension with unmatched velocity. All will benefit from an accelerated mind, if only they open their minds to the grand possibility.

Within your range of authentic potential lies a supreme being—an intellectual Hercules. Through intensive research and design of data in the computer, we've created an entity capable of amazing functions. Our generation has the ability to devise a machine with supreme intelligence and, in the same capacity, through guided action, we have the ability to fabricate a mind with the operational efficiency of a perfectly-engineered machine with extreme ability—an identity with infinite potential and eternal possibilities. Activate your Herculean brain that lies within.

"The Mind Accelerator is a system of strategy crafted from the habits of history's greatest minds, designed to engineer tomorrow's greatest minds."
VTH

commit to greatness

This program is not meant to be ingested over the course of a few days or over a six-month period. To ensure that you experience the most remarkable transformation possible, you should progress through *The Mind Accelerator* in sequential order; start with the introduction and, not only read, but take action as you advance through each phase shift in the book.

Your journey through *The Mind Accelerator* might not be an easy one; it will demand maximum effort and commitment. Just as labour strengthens the body, it is difficulty that strengthens the mind. Without such challenge, triumph and success would cease to exist. It is in situations of adversity that you are forced to do exacting and sometimes spectacular things. "Triumphs without difficulties are empty. Indeed, it is difficulty that makes the triumph. It is no feat to travel the smooth road." To reach great heights and accomplish amazing things, we must boldly take on the challenge and not shirk when the challenge is revealed.

"With this lexicon of success you will artificially engage your inner force for success and achieve an identity of ideal proportions."
VTH

You must make a commitment to the process, forcing yourself to follow through, thereby fully utilizing the potential for growth this system offers. The cumulative effect of your thought forces will result in the discovery of those keys that will unlock your personal potential. The best things in life are always the most difficult to attain—this performance tool is an ode to that adage.

Archimedes (287-212 BC) once decreed, "Give me a lever long enough and a fulcrum on which to place it, and I shall move the world." This book is your lever; placing its strategy upon your mind will power your abilities and give you the strength to shake the world. If you have the desire to rewrite history, spark a revolution of change in thought, lead the world's largest company, be elected president of your native country, invent a cure for cancer, help the impoverished of the world, develop an alternative energy source, or become a working professional, it begins here. With *The Mind Accelerator* firmly pressed in your potential-laden hands, the journey begins now.

"You may delay, but time will not."
Benjamin Franklin

12 Days to accelerate your mind

SPEND THREE DAYS ON EACH PHASE OF *THE MIND ACCELERATOR*—72 HOURS OF FOCUS ON EACH PHASE OF PROGRESSION, AMOUNTING TO A **12**-DAY PERIOD OF SELF-RESURRECTION. BEGIN THIS QUEST AND REVOLUTIONIZE YOUR MIND.

The ***Mind Accelerator*** *v.1*

your lexicon for success

Taylor Andrew Wilson

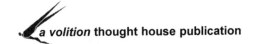
a volition thought house publication

T H E   M I N D   A C C E L E R A T O R   V . 1
BRAIN   TECHNOLOGY   BY   VOLITION   THOUGHT   HOUSE   INC.   FIRST   EDITION
WRITTEN   BY   TAYLOR   ANDREW   WILSON,   CEO   VOLITION   THOUGHT   HOUSE   INC.
PUBLISHED & DESIGNED BY VOLITION THOUGHT HOUSE INC., LONDON. PUBLISHED SIMULTANEOUSLY IN U S A

| www.TheMindAccelerator.com |

Attention Corporations, Education Boards, and Educators:

The Mind Accelerator is a powerful tool that will revolutionize the way your organization and the people within it function. This manual of higher functioning is available at quantity discounts with bulk purchases. For general information, consulting inquiries, reseller information, licensing, promotional material or any other inquires please contact us:

Volition Thought House Inc. HEADQUARTERS
517 McCormick Blvd.
London, ON
N5W 4C8
CANADA

Volition Thought House Inc. USA
1133 Broadway, Suite 706
New York, NY
10010
USA

email: contact@volitionth.com
website: www.volitionth.com

National Library of Canada Cataloguing in Publication Data

Wilson, Andrew Taylor
        The Mind Accelerator : your lexicon for success / by Taylor Andrew Wilson

ISBN: 0-973-19710-2

1. increase IQ 2. improve reading 3. success 4.Volition Thought House 5.Title

Table of Contents

Introduction

Since the dawn of time, the galactic mesh of molecular elements and atomic matter that define our universe have been fixed and constant. But these atomic energies that bind our universe are in a constant state of flux—moving cyclically through their paths of existence, their composition in a continuous state of change, being reformatted by interstellar explosions and chemical reactions. Matter is never extinguished, nor destroyed—only changed. A carbon atom that was once part of an asteroid may soon become part of earth's ozone, which is in turn photosynthesized by flora and cycled through the lungs of fauna. Every planetary organism shares this cyclic existence—physical life forms die and turn to ash, only to become part of the earth, to provide nutrients and nourishment to future organic generations.

"The human organism is not only a product of the universe, but is a universe in itself."

VTH

Every molecule in our bodies contains matter that was once subjected to the superb temperatures and pressures at the core of a star—from which the iron in our red blood cells originated. The oxygen we breathe, the carbon and nitrogen in our tissues, and the calcium in our bones were also formed through the fusion of smaller atoms at the centre of a star.

In a sense every individual has been in a star; in a way each human has been in the vast empty spaces between the stars; and—if the universe ever had a beginning—each of us was automatically there. This is the law of existence: the very law that fuses space and time into the fabric of our universe, and the very law that accounts for the reality in which we've come to exist.

"The gem cannot be polished without friction."

Chinese proverb

Since this theoretical conception of the universe, since the beginning of time, never has matter been so perfectly formatted. Never has atomic mass and energy been aligned in such a way as to create such a special creature. A divine providence has placed a certain power upon the shoulders of humankind, namely, to be one with the rational purpose of the universe. In the human species, the universal flow of atomic matter has evolved into a truly magnificent specimen.

genius is to be made

Every instant of every moment, a beautiful human mind is born—a mind that has the power to inspire miraculous transformations and forever alter the fundamentals of our world— a mind with the potential genius to enact change and redefine existence. This limitless potential of the mind is the human gift, the trait that draws a strong distinction between humankind and all other species and sets us apart from the rest.

The human system is inherently programmed for success-minded brilliance, and supreme intelligence is hard-wired within our DNA; but it exists only as potential—potential that must first be accessed and activated. As an organism of the universe, we arrive into this world as diamonds in the rough, i.e., unrefined entities. A brilliant mind is an inherent quality that must be brought forth. With courage, relentless pursuit and grand character, a beautiful mind must be built. The critical height of genius must be constructed. The diamond within can only be made to sparkle at its full potential with friction.

14

Those who attract success, fraternize with achievement and go on to build brilliant minds undergo a second adolescence. They come to a stark and sobering realization: "I don't know, so I must seek to find out." Geniuses recognize that there is more to life than that which they've already discovered—more to being and living than that which they already know. They realize it is not enough to sit complacently with a meagre level of knowledge; they realize that remaining stagnant and ignorant to the possibility of greater things will only assure certain failure. And so, those brave enough to sense their undeveloped nature and acknowledge the prospect of a greater life generate an internal curiosity for knowledge, a strong devotion to the pursuance of that which will elevate their state of being, and wisdom that will activate a greater level of existence. Through courage and passion men and women of conviction grow to see the world in entirely new ways, transcending limits while on a journey of growth.

Genius comes by way of exploration; it is cultivated by hard work, awakened by surroundings, and sustained by determination. Genius is potential translated into action. It is realized achievement. Excellence isn't to be stumbled upon, but discovered through the self-guidance of the mind. Every individual of our era covets achievement. Every person of our time yearns to lead the most successful and pleasure-filled existence possible. But very few learn how this can be accom-

"Sheer natural genius and stunning inborn ability are gifts you must cultivate. Your genetic makeup is of little consequence—average and gifted minds alike must be developed and polished. It is the strength of your volition that determines the intensity of your sheen and the success in your veins."

VTH

plished. Those who don't live up to their potential and fail to lead successful lives do so because they close their minds to the option of greater things.

ability to redefine genius

The brilliant minds of history have defined what the term "genius" means today. Our basis of comparing intelligence and IQ is derived from certain intellects from our past: from the philosophers of the Enlightenment, thinkers of ancient Greece, composers of the Renaissance and inventors of the Industrial Age. Such celebrated individuals relied on their own self-guided depths of exploration to trigger strokes of genius and their own methods of ingenious thought, and so, only a brave few with the valour and heroism to believe in their own great mind climbed the ladder to genius.

We so often look to the past when the dynamics of the present change; literature, theatrical productions, musical compositions, artistic impressions and inventions of past times are prized jewels in our contemporary world. It is these against which we measure current advancements, inventions and revolutions. But past generations never had the strategy of Mind Acceleration; they didn't have the technology of thought that exists now. While this basis of comparison is a practical one for now, in the near future it will no longer be a reasonable one. Like no other before it, our generation has unlocked secrets of human functioning—access points to our greater mind—and thus, has gained greater entry to the infinite potential of our brain—the vast heritage to which we lay claim.

A change has been made, and just as the ignition of that first fire changed the lives and future of those who came before us, so will the distribution of this program of higher functioning. With the secrets to a greater mind accessible to today's mass population, the leaps and bounds we are poised to make will be astonishing. As the general population begins to feed upon this easily accessible information source and as the inner genius of the populace is lit, a new fire will burn brightly, forever altering the possibilities of our generation. We now exist on a performance plane that is far beyond even our greatest of ancestors. We now have the technology to break into new territory and operate in a truly infinite range. Today, we have the ability to redefine what genius means.

Phase One

LEARN ABOUT YOURSELF AND THEN BEGIN TO CHANGE YOURSELF, FOR YOU MUST FIRST ACHIEVE AN **IDENTITY PROGRAMMED FOR ACHIEVEMENT** AND CREATE A SUC-CESS-ORIENTED MENTALITY TO REALIZE SUCCESS.

Exhaustive research and study on successful scholars and elite minds has been carried out over the past century. As a result, we've developed a deeper knowledge of human behavior and ability, and uncovered fundamental prerequisites for success. As with the law of gravity, they are universal and unchanging. No individual has been known to reach critical heights of success without acting in concert with these principles of human functioning. As these principles dictate, before one can accelerate his/her mind, primary adjustments must be made.

Just as an F16 fighter jet demands fuel and preparatory work before takeoff, so do you, only in place of jet fuel, you must fuel yourself with thoughts of desire, positive belief and unlimited potential. Such fuel will stimulate evolutionary change within your mind and realign your internal structures of thought, attitude and behaviour into a mode conducive to success.

TO TAP INTO YOUR LIMITLESS MIND, TAKE ACTION ARMED WITH THIS PROVEN STRATEGY AND EXECUTE IT IN A DRIVEN MANNER. YOU MUST UNDERGO A PHASE SHIFT WITHIN. THE WINNERS OF OUR TIME HAVE TRIGGERED THIS SHIFT; THIS IS YOUR OPPORTUNITY TO DO THE SAME.

PROGRESSION SCHEDULE

Day one **Study**
    1.1 Mind Theory

Day two **Action**
    1.2 Identity Restructuring: Disarm Your Mind

Day three **Action**
    1.2 Identity Restructuring: Mind Conditioning

Mind Theory

The individual poised for accelerated functioning is a master of his internal system, enjoying an in-depth knowledge of his internal web of operational instinct, phenomena and self-concept.

The human brain boasts 6,000 miles of wiring and cabling, and is capable of processing up to 30 billion bits of information per second through its amazing 100,000-mile network of nerve fibres. A reaction in one neuron can spread to hundreds of thousands of others in a span of less than 20 milliseconds—about 10 times faster than you blink.

Cutting-edge computers can perform billions of complex computations per second—but despite the staggering amount of performance engineering that goes into today's computing technology, a central processing unit that has the ability to mimic the human mind is decades away, if not impossible to engineer. Artificial intelligence exists only in science fiction.

The human power plant is comprised of three central mechanisms, or components, that make up the greater whole. First, there is the brain stem, otherwise referred to as the reptile brain; it's the brain that we share with lower life forms such as lizards, birds and crocodiles. The brain stem controls basic functions such as breathing, heart rate and mechanisms of aggression and instinct, such as the fight-or-flight response when danger threatens—it is responsible for self-preservation and perpetuation.

"The human brain is an enchanted loom where millions of flashing shuttles weave a dissolving pattern, always a meaningful pattern, though never an abiding one, a shifting harmony of subpatterns. It was as if the Milky Way entered upon some cosmic dance."

Sir Charles
Sherrington

Second, there is the lymbic system: our emotional director and controller of hormones, thirst, hunger, sexuality, our pleasure centres, metabolism, immune functions, personal identity and important functions related to memory. The lymbic system helps maintain internal homeostasis, and is the source of the mammalian invention called emotion, such as wrath, fright, passion, love, hate, joy and sadness.

"The pharmaceutical engineer poised to invent a cure for a terminal disease, is a master of chemical and physiological theory, commanding superior knowledge of every natural law, model and formula that holds importance in his scientific field. The individual poised for success is equipped in a similar fashion."

VTH

When the superior mammals evolved into existence here on earth, the third cerebral unit was finally developed, called the neocortex. Sometimes called *thinking brain* the neocortex is a highly complex network of neural cells capable of producing a symbolic language, thus enabling man to exercise skillful intellectual tasks such as reading, writing and performing mathematical calculations. It is the great generator of ideas or, as once expressed, ". . . it is the mother of invention and the father of abstractive thought." It accounts for our intelligence and it defines human thinking and functioning.

The neocortex is our authentic resource of genius and our infinite reservoir of potential. It represents the human legacy, keeping us from an ape-like existence and distinguishes us from our ancestral genus. It is our heritage.

A million years in the making, there exists an archaeology and architecture to the thinking brain—layers of evolvement—each one designed to maintain stability in its organism as animals moved from the oceans to the land, from the savannahs of east Africa to Wall Street. Growing in size over a hundred millennia, comprising nearly both hemispheres of the brain, the neocortex has given the human race the ability to adapt to the heights of the Himalayas, the dryness of the Sahara Desert, the wilds of Borneo and even central London.

Levels of Awareness

The physical abstraction that the brain symbolizes is one of scientific wonder, but knowing the geographical mappings and physiological components of the brain isn't the answer to accelerated functioning. Knowing where feelings of love are produced won't make you better at managing it, and knowing the parts of the brain that control memory won't help you when studying for final exams. The secret lies in knowing your levels of awareness and slowly tuning your senses to command them.

It has been said that the aura of existence is an unattached state of perception, alertness and automated operation, ". . . a subjective quality of experience" that is neither here nor there. There is the internal aspect of cognition; the structure you are currently using to focus your eyes on the text and comprehend the words on the page, extending all the way to the feeling of a sharp pain from a stubbed toe, to the thoughts on the tip of your tongue.

There is also the infinite scope of mental activity that goes on just underneath this level of awareness. Actions such as walking, lifting your knees and guiding your feet up steps, or peddling a bicycle can become as automatic as breathing. And so, there also exists a part of your mind that is working undetected. This is the mind you aren't conscious of—the subconscious mind. And so, our mental state of being is said to be composed of two equally important constructs; these two mental edifices are called the *conscious* and *subconscious* mind.

The dictionary defines the term conscious to mean: awake,

"The nations of the world invest so much money and man power in exploring space, developing science, funding war, and furthering our infrastructure, that we fail to realize the leaps and bounds that can be experienced by siphoning this money into the exploration of ourselves. The payoff would be a million times greater then any other possible finding we could fund."

VTH

in full possession of one's mental faculties. Your conscious mind is your purposeful and resolute level of thinking. Notable experts feel the conscious mind is the product of electric impulses, broadcasting an electromagnetic field from the mind. When we see an object, signals from our retina travel along nerves as waves of electrically-charged ions, and as they reach the nerve terminus, the signal jumps to the next nerve via chemical neurotransmitters.

"One man who has a mind and knows it can always beat ten men who haven't and don't."

George Bernard Shaw

In this way, electrical signals are processed in our brain before being transmitted to our body. But where, in all this movement of ions and chemicals, is consciousness? Scientists can find no region or structure in the brain that specializes in conscious thinking. This entity that defines the human condition–and is as absolute as the earth we stand on–remains a mystery.

Language, creativity, emotions, spirituality, logical deduction, mental arithmetic, and our sense of fairness, truth and ethics, are all inconceivable without consciousness. You use it when you talk on the phone, when you write a test, when you work on the computer, when you converse with your family and when you tie your shoelaces.

Generally speaking, the conscious mind allows us to be aware of that which is felt or experienced within our mind and being, causing us to be aware of that which we perceive outside and inside ourselves. It is the part of our mind that accounts for perceptual experience, bodily sensation, mental imagery, emotional experience, occurring thought and much more. Visualize a vivid green meadow, the Eiffel Tower, or a Lamborghini Diablo. Simulate the feeling of deep regret, a sharp jolting pain, the sensation of a pleasant surprise, the sadness of melodramatic cinema, the fluttering energy of being in love, the sweet smell of fresh cookies, or the deep and heavy weight of irksome angst. All of these emotionalized thoughts, feelings and sensations are part of your conscious level of thinking—your inner life of the mind.

"Conscious-ness is only the 'prover-bial tip of the iceberg'."

VTH

Your conscious mind is your deliberate level of thinking, responsible for collecting information from the environment and transferring it to the subconscious, and subsequently making rational decisions. It acts as a filter of experience and perception, shuttling that which it feels to be true and relevant to the subconscious, and rejecting that which is out of sequence with your conscious reality. It has been said to be the planner and director of your life; all that you know and all that you feel, and it's completely responsible for that which you are.

Case In Point
The Discovery of the Subconscious

At the turn of the century (1895) Dr. Emile Coue broke new ground in affirmation techniques, curing patients in Europe and North America with recovery rates 5 times faster than any other hospital in the world. His simple yet powerful affirmation was: "Every day, in every way, I am getting better and better." He taught his patients to repeat this affirmation for two minutes each morning and evening. That's all, but the results were dramatic. This breakthrough led to the discovery of the true power that the subconscious mind holds.

Your subconscious is the hardware of your mind, your mental hard drive. Today's most radical mainframes can't even take into account one percent of what this built in, between the ears organism instinctively, involuntarily, and instantaneously takes into account. For every thought, awareness or impression you consciously have, you experience hundreds more at the very same instant, in your subconscious.

Your subconscious mind has a homeostatic impulse within your physical being—it keeps your body 98.6 degrees Fahrenheit, your heart rhythmically beating, and your lungs pumping. Paralleling this obvious task is the subconscious homeostatic impetus of your mental realm. It always works in harmony and consistency with your emotionalized thoughts, hopes and desires. It is subjective, meaning it simply obeys the commands of your conscious mind. Your subconscious keeps you thinking and acting in a style and mode consistent with your past, your programmed comfort zones and your consciously determined strengths and weaknesses. Our habits of thought, especially the thoughts that we don't even consciously think any more, control every action and emotion we have... even in our sleep. Programmed within our subconscious is our self-concept; the compass or homing beacon of our internal reality, and the source code of our self identity.

Self-Concept

By simple definition, our self-concept is the totality of a complex, organized and dynamic system of learned beliefs, attitudes and opinions that we hold to be true about our personal existence. It's our personal bundle of beliefs. If the conscious mind is the programmer, and the subconscious is the hard disk, than one's self-concept is the operating system.

What this means is that we react to our external world in terms of the way we perceive this world. This perception is shaped by our self-concept, but individuals are not always aware of their absolute, true, or actual self—only of their own concepts and perceptions of themselves. We behave, not in accordance with reality, but in accordance with our *perception* of reality. How we feel about ourselves is all that's important, for all that we will ever accomplish is determined by our individual self-concept.

Your self-concept dictates your beliefs and, thus, generates and predicts your performance and conduct in all ways of your life. It is your frame of reference through which you interact with the world. Everyone perceives reality through a different filter, as everyone has a unique concept of themselves, and how they fit into the world around them. You will never find yourself acting in a way that contradicts this framework. You are simply unable to see things in any other light, and your behavior will always be consistent with your self-concept. You have gotten where you are, and are what you are, because of what you believe yourself to be. Think of your self-concept as a winding path; on the walk of life, you will never deviate far from this pre-set, marked path of self-conception.

Your external self is a manifestation of your internal self and cannot be otherwise. Woodrow T. Wilson, former president of the United States, said: "All the extraordinary individuals I have known were extraordinary in their own estimation." You are only valued in this world at the rate you desire to be valued. You walk the way you walk, talk the way you talk, think the way you think, dress the way you dress, look the way you look, and act the way you act each day as a result of the value you attach to yourself. These factors of interaction with your outer world reflect your inner organism; you cannot become the high-achieving individual you covet, without first changing your central operating system, your inner beliefs, your self-concept.

Your self-concept cuts across, and encompasses every other variable of your being (motives, needs, attitudes, values, personality), thus creating a central, root variable which you can manipulate, allowing you to change nearly every aspect of your internal self. Every negative and positive trait you have is rooted in this internal mechanism.

Your self concept, comfort zones, or mental grooves are formed and worn over time by your dominant conscious habits, and thoughts. You will always feel awkward and out of place, the farther you push yourself out of these grooves. The middle of your groove is where you are right now; it reflects what you do day-to-day. As you move closer to the edge of this groove, or to the wall, you are slowly moving outside of your comfort zone. For many, a wedding toast, or group presentation may be near, or on the other side of this wall, making it difficult for them to perform.

At the end of the day, it is these grooves that dictate whether you're second rate or a champion. The most successful individuals scale these walls as they approach them, consistently breaking through to new ground. They push through these psychic boundaries, and widen their grooves, realigning their comfort zones, and activating personal growth. By choosing your habits, you determine the grooves into which time will wear you. The more you work to expand your grooves, the more your life will become enriched with happiness, success, and achievement. Just as a rubber band can be stretched and refitted, your comfort zone can be molded to reflect any change or growth you undergo in your conscious realm.

You may feel uncomfortable or inadequate your first time in a new athletic sport, job setting, or training program, but as you slowly break free from your old habitual ways of thinking and acting, your subconscious mind will adjust and strengthen. You will slowly become more comfortable in your new situation, until you begin think thoughts of confidence and competence. And this is when the growth and mastery occur.

It's easy to do nothing—it's easy to choose not to push the limits of your comfort zone. But by making this choice, you will be perpetually stuck in a low achieving station. Realize that, if it's worth doing successfully, than it has to be worth doing badly until you develop a feel for it—until you cultivate a new comfort zone at a more advanced level of competence. The key to unbounded personal evolution is this: change your self-concept, to change your life.

Case In Point

Earl Nightingale, author of *The Strangest Secret*, often told of his visit to the Great Barrier Reef. This wonder of the world stretches nearly 1,800 miles from New Guinea to Australia. Noticing that the coral polyps on the inside of the reef, where the sea was tranquil and quiet in the lagoon, appeared pale and lifeless, while the coral on the outside of the reef, subject to the surge of the tide and power of the waves, were bright and vibrant with splendid colours and flowing growth. Earl

Nightingale asked his guide why this was so. "It's very simple," came the reply, "the coral on the lagoon side dies rapidly with no challenge for growth and survival, while the coral facing the surge and power of the open sea thrives and multiplies because it is challenged and tested every day. And so it is with every living organism on earth."

An Overview

Your conscious mind is the deciding director of your life, and your subconscious mind makes your actions consistent with the information that we have accepted as true in our conscious mind.

Your Conscious Mind

Your deliberate level of thinking, responsible for collecting information from your external environment, storing it in your subconscious, and making rational decisions. It's the planner and programmer, and is completely responsible for directing your life.

Your Subconscious Mind

Your unconscious level of thinking and hard disk, responsible for autonomic body control such as breathing and heart beat, the storage of information in the so-called memory bank (it records every experience) and goal seeking (it can be programmed to seek a target). Your subconscious holds your personal bundle of beliefs; those of which you hold about yourself and the external world, forming the very fabric of your universe. It is changing this fabric that will lead to revolutionary change in your existence.

Your Self-Concept

Your self-concept exists within your subconscious—it's the totality of a complex, organized, and dynamic system of learned beliefs, attitudes and opinions that you hold to be true about your personal existence. It's your personal bundle of beliefs. If the conscious mind is your programmer and the subconscious is your hard disk, then self-concept is your operating system.

Belief for Success

"This life is worth living, we can say, since it is what we make it."
William James

It has been proven over the past millennia that your ability to act successfully, and garner personal achievement is dependent on your internal patterns of conscious thought. All that you accomplish or fail to accomplish is the direct result of your own thoughts.

Take a quick study of the lives of those illustrious men and women who shook the world, and made it better and you'll realize the one common thread that is interwoven within all their lives. These high-achieving people all seemed to hold an unshakable belief in their ability to overcome all obstacles and reach great heights; every thought that emanated from their minds was one charged with positive energy.

They believed so strongly in themselves that they were able to accomplish amazing goals, always able to rebound after failure and continue their mission of excellence. Just as a motor runs more efficiently and needs less fuel to run smoother and faster when the pistons and cylinders are in perfect alignment, you perform better when your beliefs, thoughts, expectations and goals are in synch with that which you want to accomplish.

Psychology's First Law

It was only 150 years ago, that the very crux of individual prosperity was isolated and identified. Although it has taken nearly forever to realize, it has forever existed and has forever been within the lives of us all—past and present—always working for us or against us, but in a largely unidentified capacity.

What is this first law? In scientific terminology it can be described many ways, but stated simply: "You get more of that which you reinforce." Embedded within the many strata of this age-old theory, the following Maxim of Belief is a product of this hard-earned truth.

The Maxim of Belief

This maxim alone has the power to change your very existence. If you can only inject this keystone of human behavior into your mind, and let it guide your actions, you will undergo limitless change.

"I think, therefore I am."
Rene Descartes

This maxim states that what you believe with feeling and conviction becomes your reality. A biblical passage articulated this principle; "According to your faith, shall it be done unto you." William James, MD, of Harvard said "Belief creates the actual fact." Henry Ford pronounced, "If you believe that you can do a thing, or if you believe you cannot, in either case, you are right." In summation, you are what you believe you are.

Every great success story began by somebody first believing

it to be possible- but we do not always believe what we see, rather, we often see what we believe. Over 99 percent of the global population holds erroneously permuted beliefs about themselves, and their external world within their subconscious. Nearly all individuals are delusional in some capacity. We may believe ourselves to be incapable when we truly are capable, we may think that everyone else is more effective when they truly aren't, and we may deem the entire economy incapable of giving us a break when it truly is. The world is our oyster, but it will only give us pearls if we believe them to be there. Your external reality will always match your internally held beliefs, however falsely based they may be.

"To accomplish great things, we must not only act, but also dream; not only plan, but also believe."
Anatole France

By changing your beliefs, you will change your reality. Whatever new belief you may be trying to adopt, if you can believe in it strongly enough, it will become your truth. Once you are able to change the perception you hold of yourself, you will effectively become that new person—for better, or for worse.

This is a universal law, and all humans are incapable of acting against it. The human mind is unequipped to act outside of its internally held beliefs. If you believe that jumping off a 50-foot cliff may injure you, than you will never jump off a 50-foot cliff unless pain is your intention. If you truly think that staring at the sun will burn your retina, then you will never stare at the sun. If you believe tap water to be unsanitary, you may always drink bottled water and if you believe football to be dangerous, you may never play the sport. But how do you know for sure that the sun is damaging to your eyes? Because scientific research has proven it. Well, has scientific research proven that you are unable to become an extremely wealthy individual? Has it been proven that you cannot become that next great success story?

You operate in harmony with internal thoughts that you have come to think of as true. By forming personal beliefs about what you are and are not capable of, then you naturally constrain and limit your effectiveness. You may never commit to a physical training regimen, if you believe yourself destined for obesity and hopelessly overweight for life. Conversely, you may always work in labour-intensive jobs if you believe yourself to be mentally inadequate for anything else. These simple beliefs about what you excel in, and what you are poor at effectively dictate how well you perform. Regardless of your true mental capacity, if you believe you are unsuited for a 'desk job' then your subconscious mind will work to create actions that support this. At the first sign of challenge or difficulty, you simply will not go the extra mile needed to succeed in a mentally-demanding situation. Perhaps you received poor grades in school and, as a result, you formed a powerful belief that you lack mental ability or the discipline to develop your mind, so you simply give up. In the words of Charles F. Kettering, American engineer and inventor, to succeed we must ". . . believe and act as if it were impossible to fail."

Case In Point

An average, educated 35-year-old man was down on his luck; he had just been fired, was recently divorced, and felt completely, mentally wasted. He had absolutely nothing to lose, and at his wits end, decided to go see a local psychic. During the reading, she told the man that he was the reincarnated spirit of Napoleon Bonaparte, the great emperor of France. The man was astonished; he couldn't contain his adulation— he truly believed in the fortune teller's prophecy.

He began to walk and carry himself like the great French emperor, beaming complete confidence. He spoke and gestured in a grandiose, assertive manner. He developed a heightened sense of self-importance, and believed he had the abilities of the great French militarist and tactician. He quickly got a new job, and rose through the ranks. His life improved completely in every way—financially, socially, and spiritually—within a few short months. His belief was so strong, that since the time of his reading, his life began to change completely. His self-concept was transformed instantaneously and his external reality was quickly revamped to match the metamorphosis. Soon after, through discussion with friends, and some research as well, he discovered that he was most likely not Napoleon reincarnate; he was fooled by the psychic. But it was already too late; his self-esteem, and attitude had been completely revamped, and he continued to carry that heightened self-concept. He unceasingly achieved and succeeded from that moment on; nothing could stop him; he had propelled himself onto the perpetual path of success, and his momentum, desire, and self-beliefs were sky-high.

"If you can imagine it, you can achieve it. If you can dream it, you can become it."

William Arthur Ward

If you believe you are going to succeed, then you probably will. Mohammad Ali is often regarded as the greatest sports figure who ever lived. As well as his obvious talent, strength, stealthy speed and courage, the main reason he was so great was his tremendous self-belief. His expectations and confidence were sky-high. Most of us have seen television clips of Ali during his boxing years, claiming he was the greatest. When he told everyone this, was he the greatest? No, at that time, he still had a lot to prove. What he did have though was complete belief in his own ability. That belief was soon reflected in his performance, beating Joe Frasier to become the heavyweight champion of the world. Despite being stripped of his world title in 1967, because he would not fight in the Vietnam War, he was not deterred. He came back seven years later, won the title again, and proceeded to keep it for another four years. His belief that he was the greatest, took him not only to the pinnacle of boxing, but to the pinnacle of sport as a whole. Mohammad Ali has shown that, ultimately, those who win are those who know they can.

"Whether you believe you can do a thing or not, you are right."

Henry Ford

You can improve personal performance in all aspects of your life, by simply changing the beliefs you hold about yourself. By developing the absolute sense of conviction that mighty beliefs provide, you can achieve virtually anything, including those things that others may be convinced are impossible.

Case In Point

A European venture capitalist had championed two globally-successful corporate undertakings and scored millions in profits through real estate dealings. He was the man of the moment, but in one fell swoop the economy fell out from under him—wiping away his fortune and leaving him in debt, right back at square one—since graduating from university a decade earlier, he had not made any net financial gain; only net loss. Looking at his assets and tangible resources, there was nothing that separated him from the green university graduate he was ten years earlier, except for one thing. He had the self-concept of a winner—he had the internal environment of a wildly successful business magnate.

Whether his external environment supported that internal belief was no matter because, at the end of the day, month or year, it would. Within 18 months he climbed his way back to the top, and claimed achievement once more.

By implementing Phase 1 of this book, following through the phase shifts of mind acceleration, and truly believing in the power these strategies hold for self-change and growth, you will begin to travel the road of success. The Belief Maxim will soon work for you, not against you—and your true potential will begin to reveal itself.

Continue on, and learn how tremendous self-belief and positive conscious thought can be besieged, and deterred by Self-Destructive Beliefs—subconscious destructors of successful action.

Self-Destructive Beliefs

From childhood, each and every one of us—throughout our formative years and finally in adulthood—weaves our own intricate web of self-concept; these beliefs are not innate, but born in response to every thought and experience (especially interpersonal experiences), every humiliation and triumph, every loss and win we experience. Each of us has developed a self-identity concerning every talent, every characteristic and every situation in which we might find ourselves.

This vision and light in which we see ourselves is constructed in response to external influences and stimuli. All significant experiences in our lives affect how we view ourselves. The process of interaction with the external world and reflection on our performance, provide the foundation of our self-concept; both how well we think we did and how well others affirm we did have great influence on our beliefs.

We also compare ourselves to the performance, attributes and accomplishments, or lack thereof, of those people around us. For this reason, sibling rivalry can be a major influence on our lives. If we are constantly being compared to an older, higher-achieving brother/sister, it can inspire feelings of incompetence, or inability. An emotional trap such as this will provoke serious feelings of dismay and insipidness.

This variance in factors combines to cause a subjective and slanted self-analysis, ultimately resulting in negative beliefs, such as, "I'm not smart enough," or "I'm incapable of . . ." These self-sabotaging notions are based purely on false information, not fact. As Mark Twain, one of America's greatest writers, once said: "The most difficult thing is, we do not deal in facts when we are contemplating ourselves." These thoughts are Self-Destructive Beliefs that resonate from our minds' inner voice. This negative presence is a cyst, an internal rot of negativity and source of pessimism for every individual—a malignant tumour of varying proportion that often proves the arch-enemy of success and achievement.

According to Freudian psychoanalysis, it is within the subconscious that repressed memories of negativity are stored; memories of bad experiences that greatly influence our conscious behaviour, even though we are unaware of their impact. Self-Destructive Beliefs emerge from our subconscious; they pin us down and bar us from meeting our peak potential. They generate corrupting habits and are the reason for much of the failure in our lives. They are virtually always based on fictitious, over-exaggerated information and false impressions that we have accepted as true.

Negative beliefs encompass a wide array of personal convictions. Often they remain unnoticed, silently destroying our self-concepts.   The most extreme and debasing Self-Destructive Beliefs occur in those individuals who demonstrate irresponsibility, a fear of failure, and who fall prey to destructive criticism.   Self-Destructive Beliefs are like steel plates sawing through our every thought and effort.   They are the brakes of our lives.   They slow us down, sap us of positive momentum and decelerate our advancement—just the same as driving with the emergency brake on.   Negative mental habits begin as cobwebs, develop into cables and take hold of our lives.   We might never be physically limited or restricted, but we may have made our own prison.   Just as intricate viruses attack the operating system and hard drive of your computer, Self-Destructive Beliefs are the largest threat to a healthy self-concept.

Ultimately, the adoption of these counterfeit beliefs results in a skewed and untrue self-concept and a tainted subconscious belief structure—but, herein lies the answer to our salvation, a simple insight that will change our world and initiate our ascension to the top.

Due to the dynamic and subjective quality of your subconscious, it can be readily changed and altered through the directed focus of thought.   Thousands of documented studies highlight how individuals have effectively enhanced their self-concept and internal belief structure.   It is something that cannot be done by simply willing it to happen.   It takes dedicated, directed action.

It is truly impossible to realize your potential unless you eliminate Self-Destructive Beliefs from the equation.   Recent research has proven that approximately 87 percent of the things we say to ourselves are negative, self-destructive, undermining thoughts. Imagine the condition your mind would be in if you were conditioned to operate just like the average North American (the odds say you are)? Imagine the improvement your life would undergo if you learned how to reduce this number by a mere five percent or more. Remember, the only limits to your personal success are self-imposed. Learn what these restricting beliefs are, and how to eliminate them.

1. Accept Total Self-Responsibility

The growth from immaturity to maturity has a lot to do with realizing that you are fully responsible for your life and for everything that happens to you. Where you are today is the lump sum of every choice you have made—both good and bad—leading up to this moment. You are exactly where you are right now because that's where you choose to be.

Trying to rationalize or argue away total personal responsibility will accomplish nothing, except stop you from assuming responsibility for your life and future. That would mean you've surrendered self-control and effectively created a cyst of negative emotion within your metaphysical realm—a cyst that multiplies in size and breeds underachievement.

Accepting responsibility is not optional; recognizing your "response-ability." your ability to respond and choose your response, is paramount to your success. The minute you undertake personal responsibility, you stop placing blame on others. In reality, the only person you can blame is yourself; the realization that you are either at fault or deserve credit for all the success and failure you've undergone will release the negative energy locked within you and will begin to enhance your potential.   In the words of Jim Rohn, author and businessman: "You must take personal responsibility. You cannot change the circumstances, the seasons, or the wind, but you can change yourself. That is something you have charge of." The high-achieving individual realizes that everything in life is optional—even being alive. Say to yourself: "Everything is up to me and for me I will be held responsible!"

Grasp Control

A part of personal responsibility lies in accepting the power of choice. You've held this power from a very young age, whether you realized it or not; everything you've accomplished, failed at and experienced in your life has been your choice. You are not a victim of society and external happenings, but the product and sum of your past choices. Victims never achieve: they're too busy laying blame and holding refuge in a sphere of malevolence and self-loathing. Accepting this is the first step to total responsibility.

Forgive yourself and those around you for their choices; for you and everyone else are only human. The following is a prescribed structure which groups those people in your life into three different categories for you to address.

1st: Forgive your parents

Understand that your parents are just human beings. Whenever you think negative thoughts about your parents, tell yourself that you forgive your parents 100 percent. You'll soon begin to relate to your parents as friends and adults, and you will no longer feel like a victim of circumstance.

2nd: Forgive everybody else

"As human beings, we are endowed with freedom of choice and we cannot shuffle off our responsibility upon the shoulders of God or nature. We must shoulder it ourselves. It is our responsibility."
Arnold J. Toynbee

"Success on any major scale requires you to accept responsibility . . . in the final analysis the one quality that all successful people have . . . is the ability to take on responsibility."
Michael Korda, author and editor-in-chief of Simon & Schuster

Accept full responsibility for your life and understand that you are at least partially responsible for most injustices. You do not have to like the person you forgive; you just have to forgive them by understanding that they are simply human. Harbouring feelings of resentment and blame is like taking a pill and waiting for the other person to die—it simply doesn't make sense. As the Chinese proverb puts it: "When you seek revenge, dig two graves—one for your enemy, one for yourself."

3rd: Forgive yourself

Realize you make mistakes, learn from them and then forgive yourself. Accepting responsibility looks to the future and assigning blame looks to the past.

"The price of greatness is responsibility."

Sir Winston Churchill

Once you can eliminate outward hate, you will stop the ceaseless pointing of that same finger at yourself. Breaking this negative pattern will elevate you to a more effective level of existence. You will have released a great deal of negative energy from your mind by eliminating the first of three core negative beliefs. You'll feel a surge of energy and a growing hunger to accomplish your dreams as you recognize that you are responsible for both your present and your destiny.

Put into action your conscious choice. Whenever you find yourself laying blame and fault and not taking responsibility for your problems, substitute that thought for the thought, "I am responsible." With effective execution, this principle will activate feelings of duty and control and you will feel immeasurably better for it. Assuming control and responsibility over your life is a huge step towards achievement. All success-minded individuals prefer to be accountable.

2. Accept and Embrace Failure

We are all born into this world without a self at all. We are pure potential. We have no sense of our strengths or weaknesses, no positive or negative habits. This is clearly illustrated as we witness the conduct of children; they never become embarrassed and are completely fearless. They cannot discriminate between wrong and right, true or false, safe or dangerous. Children virtually do anything, say anything and try anything. A parent's job is to be not only a caregiver, but a bodyguard; they have to keep their kids from doing great harm to themselves, as they are completely fearless. Children don't fear social settings, they don't hate learning and they never shy away from new things. Henry David Thoreau described the human natural impulse when he said, "Men are born to succeed, not to fail."

Over time and in due course, fears are constructed as children watch their parents, siblings and others interact. They may observe a parent who carried a negative attitude towards school and dropped out. They may see their mother stress and fret over hosting family, or their father's apprehensions for learning a new skill or trying a new field. As children, all we know is to mimic our parents, and so their strain of thinking becomes imprinted in our minds.

Similarly, if we as children are continually told, "No, you can't," or "Don't," all we learn is that trying new things elicits a negative response. Children can only accept this negativity as true. As Freud's pleasure/pain principle dictates, all humans act toward pleasure and avoid pain. In consequence, fear and restraint becomes ingrained into children's subconscious minds and this controls their actions for the rest of their lives.

"I am responsible. Although I may not be able to prevent the worst from happening, I am responsible for my attitude toward the inevitable misfortunes that darken life. Bad things do happen; how I respond to them defines my character and the quality of my life. I can choose to sit in perpetual sadness, immobilized by the gravity of my loss, or I can choose to rise from the pain and treasure the most precious gift I have—life itself."

Walter Anderson

For these reasons, by the time we reach our formative years, most of us have developed a *fear of failure*. Research has proven that this Self-Destructive Belief is the greatest obstacle that stands between you and success. It stops you from trying new things, experiencing new feelings and venturing into uncharted territory. The trouble this causes is that, without weathering difficult situations, you will never experience meaningful accomplishment; without tackling situations you may fear, peak success will never be attained.

Influential author Dale Carnegie once said: "Most of the important things in the world have been accomplished by people who have kept on trying when there seemed to be no hope at all." What many of us don't realize is that the most successful people fail the most. Einstein, Edison . . . every great individual has failed more than he has succeeded; but the one time things went right, everything changed. Those great thinkers who were once viewed as fanatical eccentrics had become great geniuses and were no longer great failures. In today's society the distance between insanity and genius is measured only by success; fortunes can change and destinies can transform in an instant, but only for those who try. Here is one thing that is guaranteed: every individual you encounter who has enjoyed more success and reached a higher station than you has experienced more failure than you.

To fail is to successfully learn what doesn't work. Failing an exam shows you how not to study, while writing a poor essay indicates what you ought not do next time. The lessons that failure provides are always integral to your further development. You live your whole life in the future and the more you fail now, the more knowledge and wisdom you gain for that future. Just as your odds of hitting a baseball improve after every swing, your odds of success improve after every failure. In the words of US Senator Robert Francis Kennedy: "Only those who dare to fail greatly can ever achieve greatly." To succeed is to fail first.

Eliminating the fear of failure is integral within any profitable corporation. To succeed as an entrepreneur or a corporate executive is to take calculated risks and accept failure. Dan Scheinman, a Cisco vice-president, recently voiced: "If you hit five out of five, you won't do well here. People like that aren't taking enough chances. If you hit eight out of ten, that's the Cisco way."

"Cowards die many times before their deaths. The valiant never taste of death but once."
William Shakespeare

With technology changing so fast, successful companies are the ones that take risks on new products and get them to market fast. More careful, risk-averse companies get left in the dust. Put simply, the fast beat the slow. This is the iron law of the new economy. Even a giant company like Microsoft can be slain. No company is powerful enough to derail the onrush of venture capitalists who are fueled by a steady stream of new technology, while taking the right risks.

Just like every environment, the technological world is a culture of abundance with lots of rewards to go around for the winners. These rewards drive the risk-taking machine, but you can be sure that they don't go to all. Nearly every business mogul has had the experience of failure and has had to subsequently bounce back to claim success and wealth. For those in the new economy, risk-taking and experiencing failure are prerequisites for success.

A long-standing proverb says: "What you fear or expect most will surely come to pass; the body manifests what the mind harbours." Under-achieving individuals have mastered the habit of concentrating on the failure they've experienced in their lives; they are always reliving those moments, thus reinforcing the losing cycle. Whether it be remembering a poor grade when writing your final exam, or reliving that failed job interview just before your next one. All that you will achieve when focusing your thought forces on previous accounts of failure, is failure.

Many underachieving individuals also tend to base their actions on external standards set by others. They set their sights too high and are unrealistic when beginning something new. For example, rather than working into a five-day-a-week fitness training program by setting small goals and slowly escalating their intensity, they will throw themselves into it with full force. They don't allow a slow transition to take place, making failure an inevitable result. After a few short weeks, they abandon their fitness plans altogether. They have not undergone the personal growth, or developed the discipline to maintain a consistent training schedule. They were motivated to build a healthier body, but motivation without the proper discipline results in failure over the long haul. They subconsciously set themselves up for failure because that is what they expected. All this approach can accomplish is to allow another memory of failure to seep into their subconscious mind and further fuel their Self-Destructive Beliefs. They propel themselves onto the path of perpetual failure by making it too hard to succeed.

Those who meet success and failure in an identical fashion—

maintain their forward advancement regardless of the outcome—are the ones who garner achievement. You must master the art of positive action. How can you change your approach to risky situations and change your beliefs of failure? Instead of building up an undefined fear, write out exactly what you are worried about in clear and concise words. Ask yourself: "What is the worst-case scenario?" And then ask yourself: "What is the best-case scenario?" Strategically attack each aspect of your failure to conquer the situation. Oftentimes, once you see it in black and white, the fear becomes much less daunting and much easier to overcome.

You must also learn to concentrate your thought forces on success by using positive language. When you think conscious thoughts, such as "I wish I could" or "I'll try," they are automatically accepted by the subconscious as failure. Your subconscious records what you say to yourself and directs your action accordingly. When you say, "I'll try," you have not committed yourself to achieving that goal. If you "hope" you'll make a million dollars, you most likely won't. You must commit to the goal by saying, "I will do it . . . I will triumph." Applying this strategy to your affirmations and truly believing in a successful outcome, you will have succeeded in breaking through a major barrier to your success; your Self-Destructive Beliefs will begin to weaken and success will become much more likely.

Don't settle for scratching in the dirt. Break free from the fear of failure and shatter the glass ceiling that has kept you from soaring with eagles. Those thoughts of fear are a trick from the enemy to steal success from you. Don't believe in fear, but rather, believe in yourself—you are destined for success. Be passionate in your desire for achievement and your fears will melt away like ice off a roof on a sunny spring day.

"I have always felt that although someone may defeat me, and I strike out in a ball game, the pitcher on the particular day was the best player. But I know when I see him again, I'm going to be ready for his curve ball. Failure is a part of success. There is no such thing as a bed of roses all your life. But failure will never stand in the way of success if you learn from it."
Hank Aaron

3. Abstain from Destructive Criticism

"Change your meaning of failure: You automatically fail if you don't try and you never fail if you never give up. Embrace failure for the new information it provides you."
VTH

A third agent of negativity and element of destruction is Destructive Criticism. Destructive Criticism arrives in two distinct forms of injurious criticism.

Derogatory Suggestion

The first form of Destructive Criticism is Derogatory Suggestion coming from others such as parents, siblings or friends. It tends to come in the form of comments such as, "Hey, fatty," "You're stupid," or "You can't do that." Encountering this type of denigration greatly diminishes your confidence and wreaks mayhem on your self-concept.

The ultimate symptom of Derogatory Suggestion is a decrease in your personal effectiveness. As you are caused to feel less attractive, less capable or more like a loser, you begin to act in that manner. Contrary to the popular phrase, "Sticks and stones may break my bones, but words will never hurt me," words *do* hurt and it's difficult to develop the thick skin needed to survive a verbal attack unscathed.

"Great deeds are usually wrought at great risks."
Herodotus

In addition, Derogatory Suggestion also initiates the development of a *fear of rejection*. You will begin to place greater emphasis on what others think of you, thus creating a negative factor in your decision-making process. You'll never do anything or say anything that may draw criticism your way; you'll never take a risk and you'll always play it safe. Those who go with the flow never go against the grain and always comply with external forces. They will never achieve the success of which they are capable.

There's always somebody saying you can't do it and those people must be ignored. As an alternative to discussing your dreams and goals openly, discuss them only with yourself—write them down and keep them private. Why? Because the vast majority of people will tell you that you will never achieve your goals. Too often, people around us, whether they be our parents, siblings or friends, put down these positive thoughts because of their own personal short-comings or cynicism. They may misunderstand your ambition as foolishness and tell you so.

You don't need the validation or accreditation of others to survive. Coming to depend on it will constrain your perform-ance. Only the healthiest, high-achieving, most rare individu-als will ever support your dreams and confirm their attainabil-ity when confronted with them. The majority will in some way speak negatively about your aspiration. Those who are great know the importance of following ambition despite the opin-ions of others. By keeping yourself out of these situations you will be better off. Don't allow yourself to keep running over the same rock day after day; you'll find yourself patching the same hole over and over, and it will only become more dif-ficult to fix. It is important to find the source of the hole and factor it out of the equation. If you have a friend who again and again makes you feel terrible through criticism and put-downs, then you are in an unhealthy environment and you should eliminate this external influence in your life by ceasing your relationship with that person. A strategic move such as this will help you to regain emotional control over that portion of your life. Powerful results come from creating an external environment that supports your desires.

It has been said that the easiest thing another person can do is criticize another human being. The great sociological

"Keep away from people who try to belittle your ambitions. Small people always do that, but the really great make you feel that you too can become great."

Mark Twain

writer, Thomas Carlyle, once said: "No sadder proof can be given of a person's own tiny stature, than their disbelief in great people."

"Ah, so you shall be misunderstood.'—Is it so bad then to be misunderstood? Pythagoras was misunderstood and Socrates and Jesus and Luther and Copernicus, and Galileo and Newton and every pure and wise spirit that ever took flesh. To be great is to be misunderstood."

Ralph Waldo Emerson

When people of this mind tell you, "You can't, you won't," it becomes absorbed by your subconscious to some extent, no matter how hard you try to ignore it; it will echo within your bones and you will have distanced yourself from that goal. The key is to keep your goals to yourself, sharing them only with those who are committed to goals of their own. You will encounter countless critics over the course of a lifetime; they exist everywhere and their primary goal is to ensure that nobody surpasses them, however useless it might be. When bumping into these types of people, keep in mind that there never has been—and never will be—a statue constructed to honor a critic.

Remember, in life there is always one surefire way to avoid criticism: try nothing, do nothing, achieve nothing. Is this really a viable option? You must trust yourself, your ability to thrive and your power to achieve. Once this is accomplished, nothing will hold you from your dreams—however impossible they might seem.

Derogatory Autosuggestion

The second form of destructive criticism is Derogatory Autosuggestion, the lack of faith in oneself and one's faculties. You have total control over this inflow of negativity, because you are the source. Derogatory Autosuggestion occurs when we say to ourselves things such as, "I'm not clever, strong or attractive enough."

Case In Point

Breaking his way into the record books is an American man who recently took on the task of climbing Mount Everest—the highest mountain in the world. Its extreme temperatures and sheer danger create an exceedingly difficult goal for even the world's best climbers. Accomplishing this task is an amazing feat, but that isn't why he is entering the record books. It's because this man is blind. In a recent interview he was asked how he did it despite his handicap, and his response was, "the barriers to success are all in your mind." He realized this powerful factor and thus immersed himself in the atmosphere of success. He thought positive thoughts and associated with uplifting individuals. He rid his internal environment of all negativity, using techniques you soon will learn.

"Any fool can criticize, condemn and complain and most fools do."
Benjamin Franklin

Eliminating Destructive Self-Criticism is one of the most effective ways there is to improve your performance sharply in a matter of days. To eliminate this form of self-sabotage, never say anything about yourself that you do not sincerely want to come true. The Belief Maxim states that your internal beliefs will soon be projected outward and form your reality. The Concentration Principle says that the thoughts you think about on a continuing basis form your beliefs and, thus, become your reality. By focusing your thought forces on malevolent feelings such as, "I won't be able to," or "I'll never be capable of," you will certainly succumb to those feelings. The destructive energy you generate within your mind will escape and become your external reality.

"To avoid criticism, do nothing, say nothing, and be nothing."
Elbert Hubbard

The strength of your capabilities and the power of your identity are strongly affected by these influences. As the principles of mental functioning dictate, all that you hear and say guides the functioning of your subconscious mind; you must deliberately use this powerful force to your advantage. Within this first phase of *The Mind Accelerator* you will make use of this phenomenon, as you learn to concentrate your conscious mind on what you want to become and begin to charge your mind with self-liberating thoughts.

High achievers get behind the wheel and take control in the driver's seat. They realize they have the power of choice, the power to take control of their thoughts and actions, for they know that ultimately they are the ones responsible for their own lives. Successful individuals relish failure and continue the pursuit with more knowledge because of it. Winners take control of their thoughts, their daily routines, their goals and their lives—they block external negative intervention and dis-regard destructive criticism. Thriving individuals create their own horoscopes and astrological forecasts. They never under-estimate the power they possess, nor do they underestimate the power of their fellow man. They spend their time suc-ceeding, knowing they have no time to lose.

Evolve

You are now aware of the dichotomy of mental powers to which you lay claim. You've discovered the importance of your self-concept—the determining factor of your ability to suc-ceed that exists within your subconscious realm. You know it's through the optimization of your self-concept that your iden-tity can evolve to a higher plane—but you've also learned about the one thing that can stop this evolution from taking place: Self-Destructive Beliefs. From it seep negative beliefs that constrain and destroy your self-concept, thus limiting your abilities and stopping you from realizing your potential.

This is why it is so important for you to silence those Self-Destructive Beliefs and minimize the effect they have on your life.

You will now be introduced to Phase 1.2: Identity Restructuring—the principle force in initiating and maintaining the flow of personal success in your life. Actively utilize this second component of Phase 1 and focus your will-power on successfully navigating this sector of internal change. Your cooperation and active participation is essential to restructure your identity effectively. No amount of financial assistance, training, guidance or effort by others will enable you to make an adequate life adjustment without your ability and willingness to utilize your total resources. You must enthusiastically invest yourself in this section; understand that changing your entire life through these processes requires a strong desire to change, a confidence that you can succeed and a feeling that you are worthy of the assistance being offered.

Through self-reflection and the concentration of your thought forces, you will come to view yourself in a new, more powerful way. You will discover the negative aspects of your mind. Once you recognize these Self-Destructive Beliefs through analysis and deep thought, you will begin to realize how false they are thus, allowing you to reject them and label them as wrong. Your Self-Destructive Beliefs will begin to lose their power over you and your true potential will begin to emerge from within.

You will replace these Self-Destructive Beliefs with Self-Liberating Beliefs; you can now begin to think of yourself as who you want to be; any new trait you would like to develop begins at this step in the process. By enhancing your expectations of success, beginning with the installation of new conscious thoughts, you will experience a profound attitudinal change; the impact on your individual performance and many other areas will be remarkable.

ONCE YOU BEGIN TO FOCUS YOUR MIND ON WHAT YOU WANT TO BECOME AND CAST ASIDE THOSE THOUGHTS OF SELF-DESTRUCTION, YOUR INNER THOUGHTS OF AMBITION WILL SOON CLOTHE THEMSELVES IN THEIR PHYSICAL REALITIES. REMEMBER, ALWAYS THINK HIGHLY OF YOURSELF, FOR THE WORLD WILL ONLY TAKE YOU AT YOUR OWN BEST ESTIMATE.

Beliefs: the Central Construct of Identity

Imagine waking up one day with amnesia—you have no idea who you are, what you've done, what your abilities are, and most importantly, what your limits are. You aren't labeled as average, you aren't limited by an average IQ, and you aren't categorized as an average achiever. Your whole identity has been erased from your mind—all that remains is pure, uncensored potential. There exists absolutely nothing that can stop you from attempting and trying—you are a slave to logic and *not* to conjured-up, delusional, self-sabotaging beliefs and negativity.

Perhaps you want to become influential and powerful and you feel that amassing a great deal of wealth would be the best way to achieve this. Without any trepidation at all you would begin to feed your mind with information about stocks and securities, debentures and bonds, real estate and land development. You would begin to develop relationships with people in strategic positions and individuals who control cash flow. You would take action in an unflinching manner because logic dictates that such action will bring you wealth. There is no "I can't," only strong, unswerving, forward-moving action. You can erase doubt. You can attain this mentality. You can achieve this state of mind. YOU CAN. Proceed to Phase 1.2.

Identity Restructuring

Those individuals who excel and act without compromise are able to do so because they are in complete control of their mental faculties. They know how to work smarter and utilize the power of their minds, rather than physically working harder. They've mastered the operation of both their conscious and subconscious minds and have created a supportive dynamic relationship between them, as they know this is a prerequisite to success. As a result, they attain the things they want faster and with far less effort.

"To act with confidence and courage requires tremendous internal belief in your own potential for success."

VTH

Identity Restructuring will sculpt and reformat your mind into what you want it to become. Remember, your conscious thoughts dictate your future, as well as reflect your present. By striving to focus your conscious thought forces on what you want to become, your self-concept will be bolstered and strengthened. You will generate a new set of behaviours and thought patterns, thereby dramatically enhancing your performance.

All you are and all you're capable of being is of your choosing. To enhance profoundly your likelihood of succeeding in every area of your life, to garner a bountiful future, run for president, become a financial success story, or seize your

"I know of no more encouraging fact than the unquestionable ability of man to elevate his life by conscious endeavour."
Henry David Thoreau

dreams you must activate your subconscious mind and get it to work for you rather than against you. You can either make the decision to grasp control of your personal evolution by saturating your mind with input that is consistent with what you want to become, or not. This system gives you the opportunity to make that choice. Proceed to the following system of exercises and develop a deep belief in the power your mind holds; only then will it begin to operate at the infinite scale possible.

Self-Actualization

Abraham Maslow and Clayton Alderfer, the founding individuals of humanistic psychology, developed complex theories on human motivators—Maslow's Hierarchy of Needs and Alderfer's ERG Theory. The likeness of their findings was great, and their blending provides intelligent insight into the nature of our minds.

They identified inherent needs we are motivated to fulfill. The most primary of these needs is our drive to maintain physiological balance and homeostasis. This involves the need for air, water, food, warmth and anything the physical organism needs to survive. Once these physiological needs are gratified, then our needs for safety become important. This involves security, stability, dependency, protection and freedom from fear, anxiety and chaos. Humans have a need for structure, order, law, limits, strength in the protector and so on, for these reasons. When one of these needs goes unsatisfied, it exerts a powerful effect on our thinking, thus spurring action until it is satisfied.

If these physiological and safety needs are gratified, our

relatedness needs rise to the forefront. Love, affection and belongingness become principal. Humans have a need to give and receive affection, exchange thoughts and feelings and love. When this need goes unsatisfied, the absence of friends, mates or children becomes keenly apparent. A person will hunger for relationships with people in general, for a place in the group or family, and will strive with great intensity to achieve this goal. Attaining such a place will matter more than anything else in the world; one may even forget that once, when hunger was foremost, love seemed unreal, unnecessary and unimportant. In the absence of this need, the pangs of loneliness, ostracism, rejection and friendlessness form and take hold.

Encapsulated within our needs for relatedness are our desires for esteem, accomplishment, independence and the regard of other people. All individuals in our society (with a few pathological exceptions) have a need for a stable, firmly based, typically high evaluation of themselves. We also desire self-respect. Strength, achievement, adequacy, mastery, competence, confidence in the face of the world and independence are all qualities that fulfill this need. We also desire the esteem of others. Our craving for prestige, reputation, status, fame, glory, dominance, recognition, attention, importance, dignity and appreciation are a result of this yearning. These initial levels of human needs are deemed Deficiency (D) Needs. Not satisfying these D Needs fully will leave you dead, sick or unhappy, but when satisfying these D Needs fully you will still be yearning for more. The unmitigated fulfillment of your D Needs will bring you at best a low level of superficial happiness. You will achieve the very least possible—just fighting and staving off the feelings of hunger, vulnerability, loneliness and unimportance. When remaining in the D Realm of achievement, you will never be truly happy. Even with your D Needs fully satisfied, you will soon begin to feel a new discontent and restlessness develop, because you are not meeting your potential.

One's growth must continue via the desire to gain the knowledge and understanding required to realize one's total potential. You must begin to satisfy your growth needs by acquiring the self-knowledge to develop your own authentic potential. Only when this threshold is crossed and Self-Actualization is activated, can you conquer and grasp your authentic potential. You will then and only then begin to enjoy life to the fullest and experience the elation of which you are ultimately capable. "Musicians must make music, artists must paint, poets must write" and leaders must lead if they are to be at peace with themselves. What humans can be, they must be.

"The golden opportunity you are seeking is in yourself. It is not in your environment; it is not in luck or chance, or the help of others; it is in yourself alone."
Orison Swett Marden

The only reason that the vast majority don't reach the stage of Self-Actualization is due to internal enemies. They are our barrier to progress, the brakes of our life, slowing us down, sapping us of positive momentum, and numbing our desires. They will stop us from realizing our growth needs if we don't overcome them. We must know our enemy to overcome him. The Mind Accelerator will educate you as to exactly what these barriers are. Identity Restructuring is your campaign of action: set forth to discover and overcome the dark forces and enemy outposts contained within, harness your authentic potential and engage Self-Actualization.

Progression Key

Preparing and conditioning your mind to take on a new structure of identity takes discipline and a strong inner volition for change. Remember, this system can only be as effective as you want it to be.

This is the first step in engaging your thoughts and emotions—soon they will net enough force to give you the strength to override your current beliefs. As your mental system encounters new positive messages, the state of the system will change, causing it to behave in a different way. But only through relentless repetition and consistent action can this new input penetrate and alter your self-concept.

Charge your mind, erase old outdated memories, and create a new and enhanced human operating system through the following two-part system.

Disarm Your Mind

As you now know, those Self-Destructive Beliefs that exercise a powerful hold on your day-to-day behaviour are your major barrier to progress. They emerge and tell you, "No, that will never work," or "No, you aren't clever enough, strong enough or attractive enough." They guide your behaviour and unconsciously diminish the quality of your decisions and thoughts—without your even detecting their negative influence.

"I count him braver who overcomes his desires than him who conquers his enemies; for the hardest victory is over self."
Aristotle

A mind dominated by Self-Destructive Beliefs plays it safe—it likes things to remain as they are and to stay within the comfort zone. Taking risks, changing your daily habits and

"Dismantle the governor that presently limits the abilities of your mind, for only then will performance acceleration be possible."
VTH

improving your internal sense of value will cause your mind to react by issuing self-destructive thoughts to stop you from changing.

Believe in the potential change these strategies hold for you. Your future is truly a limitless wonder, and possessing an "it'll never happen" attitude is like being locked in a cage of your own design—a cage constructed with skepticism, cynicism, ignorance and negativity. Such a thought provides a microscopic glance into the negative energy that flows through all individuals of mediocre stock. It has, is and will continue to hold you back from attaining the successes of which you are capable. As William Shakespeare once said, "Our doubts are our traders and make us lose the good we oft might win by failing to attempt." You will only begin to succeed and realize your dreams when you begin to believe and think of them as being attainable.

Reduce the power of your inner negativity by identifying its sources and its aspects of control, creating the desire to put an end to this flow of negative energy, and then disarming your mind of those agents of negativity.

Case In Point

As Napoleon Hill was finishing his book *Grow Rich with Peace of Mind*, he was visited by a master from the Himalayas. This man came from the great school of the masters, secretly residing in the Himalayas for more than ten thousand years. It has been said that these ". . . masters communicate by telepathy and can disembody themselves to travel instantly to any place they choose."

The master shared with Hill a list of what he called the 26 enemies. He said that every person, over the course of his or her life, must navigate the jungle of life where these 26 ene-mies reside. Each of us must successfully pass through our own jungle and defeat our own enemies—negative emotions.

The best way to defeat negative emotions is first to befriend them by becoming aware of them, and then owning them. The next step is to challenge them by analyzing them through questions. Once we get to know why they exist and why we feel those particular emotions, we can see the pattern we have attracted into our lives. Eliminating them becomes easier after this process.

You will need to acquaint yourself with this exercise before actually doing it. Read it through, get to know it and develop an understanding of what it encompasses. You want to get to the point where you can focus on your internal system, emo-tions and thoughts, while working through the exercise, rather than dwelling on what you should be doing and whether or not you're doing it correctly.

Step 1

As you enact the strategy in this book and join the journey of mind acceleration that it prescribes, Self-Destructive Beliefs will surface and try to throw you off kilter and disrupt your progress. The goal of this step is to locate and identify those Self-Destructive Beliefs your mind may be generating—namely, any and every thought you find yourself thinking or belief you hold that will undermine, distract and sabotage your efforts for Mind Acceleration.

To the **right** are several commonly-held Self-Destructive Beliefs that often arise in many individuals who work through

-I'm not a thinker, I'm a doer and I always will be.

-High achieve-ment and suc-cess are not possible for me.

-I'm incapable of existing at an elevated mental state.

-I'm too lazy to take the action future success demands.

-I simply don't have what it takes.

-Success takes too much hard work, and I'm not prepared for that.

the Mind Accelerator. Read through and make note of those that hold truth for you.

In the space provided (use a notepad if you need more), record 10 Self-Destructive Beliefs that have emerged from your mind in the past, those you sense now and those that you feel might emerge in the future. Create a complete compilation of every self-sabotaging thought and belief you hold that may hinder your development. Many feel the need to revisit this strategy several times as they progress through the book and notice more negative messages emerging. This step may take some time as you look inward and examine your mind. Once you've made a complete representative list of your negative inner thoughts, move on.

_____

_____

_____

_____

_____

_____

_____

_____

_____

_____

_____

_____

_____

_____

_____

_____

_____

_____

Step 2

Now close your eyes, and drawing from your list of Self-Destructive Beliefs, emotionalize and feel the past and present consequences you've experienced because of these negative beliefs. Feel the emotional cost these beliefs have had on your life. Feel what they've cost you in lost opportunities, relationships, finances, self-growth, your physical health, your level of happiness, and your level of fulfillment. What regrets have these beliefs caused you to bear? How have these beliefs held you down and stopped you from capturing that which you truly are capable of achieving?

Now visualize yourself **five** years in the future, still holding these Self-Destructive Beliefs. What has been the cost? How have they continued to hold you back from achieving your potential?

Now, step **10** years into the future, and what is it you see? Ask yourself: what has been the long-term cost of holding these Self-Destructive Beliefs?

Step **20** years into the future, and see where you have been led. Again, what is the cost?

Step 3

Return to today and come back to the present. Recognize that none of what you've imagined has happened yet. You still have control over what your destiny holds. You still have a chance to change your future and enhance its prospects.

It might have been depressing and perhaps even painful to imagine, but you've really developed a strong inner desire to

"Like Clark Kent, unbutton your shirt, shed your glasses and reveal the powerful identity of your authentic self, to the world."

VTH

ensure that this future doesn't come true. Desire is an ideal mental antidote for fear and doubt. It sparks activity, which burns up adrenaline in the system, keeps the mind busy and the hope of achievement alive. Desire is that emotional state between where you are and where you want to be. Desire triggers memories of pleasure and success and ignites the need to create new winning experiences. Desire is magnetic, positive tension. Negative tension induced by fear creates stress, anxiety, sickness and hostility; carried to extremes it can cause psychoses and death. Positive tension produced by desire is like a bow pulled taut to propel the arrow to the bull's-eye. Success is almost totally dependent on drive, focus and persistence; this exercise will give you the desire to attain those qualities.

Realize that your whole life is in the future, and changing your life right now will determine how and what you'll be in that future.

Step 4

"An affirmation is a positive, forceful statement that something is already so."

VTH

To change your future, begin to craft a list of 10 positive beliefs that not only counter your Self-Destructive Beliefs, but hit upon new areas of growth and support future actions you want to take. Decide who you want to be, what you want to be and how you want to be. Now is the time to completely redefine your identity; there are absolutely no limits or restrictions. Think of any behavioural or attitudinal quality that you would like to fuse with your identity at this very moment.

Record them below for continual future reference. There are a few new beliefs shown to the right that every human being must have installed within their system. As a reminder:

short, pithy phrases work best, but they can be as powerful as "I am capable of elevating my intelligence and capturing my authentic genius," or as short and effective as "I am smart."

I am the master of my destiny and I can do anything I can imagine.

My mind has infinite potential and once I put it to use, I will perform at genius level.

Failures are not indicators of my ability. They're simply the vital experience I need in order to learn and succeed.

I am capable of succeeding in every area of life!

I accept the impossible as the possible, the possible as the probable. Within lies a force for success that can bring me wealth, happiness and success.

Step 5

Close your eyes and visualize how these beliefs will transform the quality of your life. What will you gain by these new beliefs? How will you be socially, how will you be academically, how will you be more happy, how will you be more financially successful? How will your physical body be transformed when these beliefs begin to guide your daily actions? How will you become a more skilled competitor in the new economy?

Evaluate how your life will become greater and more fulfilling as you take recurring action and become a self-actualizer. Again, look five, then 10 and then 20 years into the future with your new beliefs. How has your destiny changed? Who will you have become?

Now is the time to decide which destiny you want, the destiny that is created with your Self-Destructive Beliefs intact, or the limitless future that is possible by eliminating them now? Make the decision and make the commitment. Create leverage over yourself. If you do not begin to change your beliefs NOW, but put it off, you may never encounter this chance again. Interrupt the pattern that negative beliefs have created and break into the realm of total achievement by moving forward to the next component.

Key to Use

Use "Disarm Your Mind" every time you sense Self-Destructive Beliefs bubble to the surface of your thoughts; add and improve the messages to counteract new sources of negativity. For the first few weeks, completing the exercise daily will reap huge benefits. The more you use it, the more change will be inspired. As growth takes permanent hold of your mind, you might wish to use the exercise only once a week.

Stratagem: The Conscious Choice

Our conscious mind can hold only one fully developed thought at a time. But what this thought consists of remains at your discretion. It can either be a positive and self-motivating thought, or a negative and self-debasing thought. The choice is yours—it can either be one or the other. You can choose to hold a positive thought, one which will push you to grow and succeed, or you may choose to hold a negative thought, one which will push you to do nothing and fail. You have the power to make that choice at all times.

You have the power to perceive any situation you encounter in a positive or negative manner. If you find yourself thinking in negative terms, force that thought out by bringing your conscious mind to focus on a positive one. Replace thoughts of worry, procrastination and self-sabotage with thoughts of hope, action and self-liberation. Put this into action and you will begin to take control of your emotional thoughts and, thus, your emotional life.

Case In Point

When a human system encounters new information, this new information changes the system, but the extent of the change depends on two key variables: the system must understand the information and the system must believe the information. If these two variables are met, the new information will transform and change the human system. Mind Conditioning will inject new information into your mind's eye—do your best to believe the power it holds; only then will you change your outlook forever.

Mind Conditioning

KEY SUCCESS STRATEGY
engage every 12 hrs

Confucius, the ancient master philosopher, once whispered: "The more man meditates upon good thoughts, the better will be his world and the world at large."

As human beings, our conscious thoughts dictate our future, as well as reflect our present. By striving to change our conscious thoughts—focusing our thought forces on who we want to become—we can set into motion a future filled with explosive accomplishment. To create change in your life, you must change your identity.

"There is nothing training can't do. Nothing is above its reach. It can turn bad morals to good; it can destroy bad principles and recreate good ones; it can lift men to angelship."

Mark Twain

As proven by study and research, the system of Mind Conditioning is the most effective method of mental programming ever discovered. Every confirmed and undeniable truth of human behavior has been integrated into Mind Conditioning. Channeling and focusing the power of your thought forces will ignite and animate your internal drive train, power—assist your actions, and thus create a forward-driving force of achievement. With consistent effort, your subconscious can become a success-generating machine.

Your thoughts must be trained and focused on a continuing basis to maintain an upward trajectory. Use the following prescribed system to maintain mental growth and charge new beliefs into your subconscious. Remember, your mind is thinking constantly and it's impossible to tell yourself once that you're an intellectual giant and have it stick—not when you follow it up with a very human mistake an hour later and the first thing you're tempted to think is, "I knew I was fooling myself! I'm no genius!"

"Ignite change in your belief in your own self-possibili-ties by immersing your mind in the impossi-bilities."

VTH

Your current beliefs took time to take root and the new ones will also take time. Think of your mind as a field. You're planting new seeds now, and with time new shoots will begin to emerge and produce fruit, but only if you give them the care they demand—only if you water, fertilize and weed your mental field each day will internal seeds of success germinate and blossom. The more you focus your thought forces on your desires, the more quickly your world will change, and the sooner you will accelerate to a success-filled future.

Adapt the Mind Conditioning strategy to your life, employ the work of the world's greatest thinkers and emulate the habits of top achievers. You will experience no greater return on investment and no greater profit from your time than the potential yield this system can create for you.

Step 1

In the most quiet and peaceful place possible, sit comfortably. Take several deep inhalations while silently saying "re," followed by several deep and slow exhalations while silently saying "lax." Breathe in with the utterance "re," and out with "lax." Continue this rhythmic mantra for a 90-second period to relax your body and prepare your mind for conditioning.

After spending approximately a minute and a half doing this, your brain will fall into the ideal state for subconscious programming, a state of narrow and relaxed mental focus, which you will learn about in greater detail later in the book. To achieve this state takes some practice and discipline, but it is completely essential, as it causes your conscious mind to be bypassed and your subconscious mind to be opened up and aligned to absorb the coming messages.

New positive beliefs and liberating thoughts will become part of your new identity at a much greater pace when in this relaxed state. After 20 Mind Conditioning sessions, you can make tremendous progress in forging a healthier, more positive, more success-calibrated persona. But if you don't properly guide your mind into its Alpha state, progress will be slowed to such a point that change may never occur. Execute this process correctly, and your mind will fall into the Alpha state, and will be ready for deep programming.

Step 2
Refer to the list of beliefs that you crafted previously. With them in your lap, sit up and read out loud those beliefs you want to become a part of your new identity and which you associate with your future success.

Remember, life is cumulative! Each time you take action in this capacity, the more power you feed your mind—with time, your mental strength will be that of a steam engine. Verbalize each formulized resolution between 10 and 30 times.

Step 3
Now close your eyes and make a picture in your mind. Visualize yourself performing, acting and succeeding with that new belief intact. Clearly visualize yourself as a successful person and acting victoriously with that new belief. Clearly see the outcome you desire, including you with your new identity and everyone else who may be involved.

Step 4

Put yourself inside the picture you've created. Use all of your senses—hearing, smelling, tasting, seeing and touching—to emotionalize the various elements of your success-filled destiny. Feel the pleasure and elation that comes with mastering these beliefs. Imagine yourself already successful and the belief already part of your identity. Create the feeling you will experience when your new identity is assumed.

Repeat step 2 to step 4 of the process for each belief, taking only 30 to 60 seconds for each.

Step 5

Exhale and confidently release all concern from your mind. Let it go, just as you would if someone you trusted said to you that you would be successful at becoming the person you aspire to be and that you shouldn't worry about it again. You will feel an overwhelming sense of purpose once you bring your mind back to its Beta state—bask in it and let it drive your actions. This is the catalyst in the process.

"A mind that is stretched to a new idea never returns to its original dimension."
Oliver Wendell Holmes

Key to Use

Use Mind Conditioning twice a day for maximum effectiveness. Perform once in the **morning** to send a strong set of signals to your subconscious mind, heightening your effectiveness for the day ahead of you, and enhancing your awareness of anything going on around you that day that could help you accomplish one or more of your goals. It will form the rudder of your day, giving you the positive momentum needed to act and perform like the new self you are shaping.

Perform once in the **evening** immediately before sleeping. You will set your subconscious to work on the last thing you think about before bed, as it usually becomes a major part of your dreams that night.

"We are what we repeatedly do. Excellence, then, is not an act, but a habit."

Aristotle

In today's fast-paced society, an extra 20 minutes a day is often hard to spare, for those who fall prey to the menial and trivial. Those who prioritize TV time over Mind Conditioning may have a difficult time making the commitment. Don't allow this to happen to you. Actions such as these are quite possibly the most important kind of action in your day. Don't put it off—there are only so many tomorrows.

Stratagem: **The Power of Focus**

Og Mandino, a celebrated and influential writer, once said, "The weakest living creature, by concentrating his powers on a single object, can accomplish good results while the strongest, by dispersing his effort over many chores, may fail to accomplish anything. Drops of water, continuously falling, hone their passage through the hardest of rocks but the hasty torrent rushes over it with hideous uproar and leaves no trace behind."

"As the human system focuses its conscious thought on new ideas, beliefs, goals and information, those new ideas, beliefs, goals and information enter the subconscious to such an extent that they become part of the human system."

VTH

Sit on the beach when it's 35 degrees Celsius and with the sun 93 million miles away. With a rudimentary magnifying glass, you can concentrate the fierce energy of the sun's rays, direct that force, centre it on one spot, and ignite a pile of leaves, causing it to burst into flames—this is a tremendous focus of energy. Everyone can focus their thought forces, zero in so totally on their personal goal or belief, concentrate their internal energy, and make it a reality. All it takes is a strong inner volition to change.

The thoughts you think about on a continuing basis become your reality. By channeling your thought forces on a quality that you want to adopt or a belief you want to attain, you will begin to accept it as realistic. Not only will it become realistic, but it will soon become possible. And once it becomes possible, you will soon consciously believe that you are able to own that quality or have that belief. Once this occurs, it will be programmed into your subconscious mind and will guide your thoughts and living existence thereafter. If you continuously focus your thought forces on the phrase, "I am a genius," your reality will begin to echo this perception. If you concentrate your thoughts on becoming extremely self-confident, after a period of time it will be so.

"Nothing can stop the man with the right mental attitude from achieving his goal."

Thomas Jefferson

Use the system of Mind Conditioning and The Power of Focus to gently guide your thought forces towards success on a continuous basis. With disciplined use, your deeds will astound you, and your performance will break barriers you previously thought unbreakable.

Identity Restructuring gives you the ability to take your life off autopilot, control your thoughts and, thus, build an inner temporal galaxy of empowering thought, effective action and unequivocal success.

Dare to call to arms the stratagem of Identity Restructuring and look upon the world with sharpened eyes and heightened senses. Notice delicate differences in the tapestry of reality and subtle changes in the framework of being, while all seemingly remains undisturbed. See how the world magically changes and yet stays the same. Begin to capture achievement, garner great success and solidify yourself on the perpetual path of success, with seemingly little extra effort or sacrifice.

"THE MOST SUCCESSFUL MEN IN THE END ARE THOSE WHOSE SUCCESS IS THE RESULT OF STEADY ACCRETION. . . . IT IS THE MAN WHO CAREFULLY ADVANCES STEP BY STEP, WITH HIS MIND BECOMING WIDER AND WIDER—AND PROGRESSIVELY BETTER ABLE TO GRASP ANY THEME OR SITUATION—PERSEVERING IN WHAT HE KNOWS TO BE PRACTICAL, AND CONCENTRATING HIS THOUGHT UPON IT, WHO IS BOUND TO SUCCEED IN THE GREATEST DEGREE."

Alexander Graham Bell

phase shift
Phase Two

When you sit in a fixed position, it may be difficult to foresee forward movement. When you live with an accustomed set of habits, it may be impossible to imagine living without them. But evolutionary law dictates that, once you ignite change and sparks forward movement, the same feeling endures. You will have a difficult time comprehending how you could exist in any other way.

CHANGE CAN GRIP PEOPLE IN SUCH A WAY AS TO TEAR THEM FROM THEIR PREVIOUS FABRIC OF REALITY—ERASING MALEVOLENT CUSTOMARY ACTION AND NEGATIVE HABIT FROM THE MIND. PERSONAL EVOLUTION CAN CATAPULT THE MIND IN SUCH A STRATOSPHERIC WAY, EFFECTIVELY JOLTING THEM FROM THEIR PREVIOUS MODE OF OPERATION, REWRITING THEIR PROCEDURAL MANUAL, AND VIRTUALLY RE-CREATING THEIR EXISTENCE, MAKING IT NEARLY IMPOSSIBLE TO IMAGINE LIVING IN ANY LESS OF A CAPACITY.

You may not be able to conceive of yourself existing on a higher plane—but once you evolve so as to exist on that plane, you won't be able to conceive of yourself existing on a lower plane. This is the law of progression.

Miles deep, underneath craggy rock and layers of granite, lies a vault of precious stone and rock—a bounty of natural wonder, an infinite resource of diamonds and gold. With the strategy of Phase 2, open your mind and mine this precious resource you hold deep within. Open your mind and let your authentic genius fly forth.

The Infinity Mind System will set fire to your nerve fibers, sparking mental growth and an increase in your IQ. You will grow to exist on a higher plane of functioning—thinking with supreme spatial awareness, strong intuitive tendencies, and a developed connection with your subconscious database.

USE THE INFINITY MIND SYSTEM TO ENGINEER YOUR iMIND.

PROGRESSION SCHEDULE

Day four **Study**

    2.1 Infinity Mind System Introduction

Day five **Action**

    2.2 Preview the Infinity Mind System

Day six **Action**

    2.2 Use the Infinity Mind System

PHASE

IMS Introduction

Visual Thinking

Ocular thoughts, visual thinking, optical ideas—limitless, unconstrained and unbounded means of thought allow us to discover otherwise impossible things. Such thinking is our brain's natural methodology of thought.

Primitive clans of human species, ancient Egyptians and aboriginal populations all communicated via pictorial representations—whether they be scratches on cave walls, hieroglyphs, intricate wall paintings, sculptures, pyramids, monuments or totem poles. This was our initial means of thought, our natural means of thought. But over time, convenience and expediency gripped much of our communications evolution.

Communication became very deliberate, defined and limited. People no longer thought in terms of hieroglyphs and pictographs, but by written words and letters. Thinking became bounded by vocabulary and by two-dimensional, text-oriented thought patterns. Prevailing forms of language shunted ideas into segments and sections, thereby realigning natural thought by breaking it up and placing it into words, sentences and pre-existing vocabulary. Emotions, ideas and

"The intuitive mind is a sacred gift and the rational mind is a faithful servant. We have created a society that honors the servant and has forgotten the gift."

Albert Einstein

lightning bolts of genius couldn't be truly articulated via verbal communication. Transferring thought into a universal medium of words and letters cut short revolutionary brain waves of ideas, as original thought cannot be communicated through unoriginal language.

This perpetual mode of articulation has surfaced universally, resulting in a loss of human potential. We think in terms of words and language in an everlasting habit of verbal consciousness. If there isn't a word for a particular emotion or thought, then such an emotion or thought isn't properly communicated, or perhaps not created at all. The dictionary of contemporary society acts as a barrier to ground-breaking and world-shattering notions.

Imagine Leonardo Da Vinci being forced to paint within a pre-defined set of lines and templates—not being able to articulate what existed in his mind, but only what the canvas allowed. If these limits had continued to be imposed upon him, pretty soon he would have grown content painting within these lines, forgetting that those limits existed at all. Original thought would automatically have been bent and shaped to fit into these templates, and Da Vinci would never have thought outside the box. The *Mona Lisa*, the *Last Supper,* and countless other products of Da Vinci's mind would not exist today if this had been the case.

Case In Point

Roman numerals were at one point the dominant method of recording numbers—a method that made adding and subtracting easy, but more complex computations such as multiplication extremely difficult—so much so that it was once considered a feat of high genius just to be able to multiply, say, XXXIV times XXVII (34 times 27).

By the sixteenth century, the pursuit of further mathematical understanding in Europe made it essential to switch from Roman numerals to the number system of the Indus Valley (a system that had been in existence since 250 BC), better known today as Arabic numerals, thereby bringing the concept of the number "zero" to mathematics.

Many Muslim mathematicians of Baghdad mastered this new mathematical methodology at its conception and soon they utilized fully the geometrical treatises of Euclid and Archimedes. Trigonometry, astronomy and geography flourished. The number system from the Indus Valley set arithmetic free, igniting a mathematical revolution. By 500 BC, mathematicians of India had solved problems that had baffled the world's greatest scholars of all time.

Hundreds of years later, sometime after Arabic numerals had been universally adopted, Carl Friedrich Gauss, the Prince of Mathematics, lamented that, had Archimedes or the rest of Europe foreseen the Indian system of numeration much earlier, how much more advanced science would have been.

The change and transformation that the adoption of Arabic numerals set forth parallels the change potential that visual thinking holds. A simple mental adjustment in thought patterns can completely revolutionize all areas of life and, thus, the progression of humanity.

the two sides of the brain

The operational dynamics of the brain help explain the effect a reduction in visual thought has on human mental perform-ance. The brain is often said to have two different hemi-spheres, the left and the right, divided by subtle functional dif-ferences. Each side is connected by the *corpus callosum*, a network of 300 million neurons that transmits specially coded neural information from one hemisphere to the other, allow-ing completely-integrated thought patterns

The left hemisphere of the brain generally specializes in rational aspects of thought, such as mathematical processes, and logical, analytical, objective and sequential thinking. It is the chief driver of language.

The right brain specializes in creative and visual aspects of thought, such as rhythm, music, visual imagery, impressions, colour and pictures. This hemisphere of the brain is much more random, intuitive, holistic and subjective. It deals with conceptual thought, and intangible ideas such as love, beauty and loyalty.

While the two hemispheres of the brain are distinguished, these differences aren't resolute nor are they definitive of the human brain. Each thought or cranial process calls in action so many different parts of the brain that each half is always being utilized—while each half holds dominion in certain areas. The two hemispheres inconspicuously work in tandem with each other, where each side make contributions based on its respective strengths, but never doing the whole job in iso-lation. Neither hemisphere is ever even moderately inactive while its counterpart completes a task alone. Instead, both make meaningful, although different, contributions to the completion of all cognitive undertakings.

Research has shown that habitually neglecting to think visually and to use your senses of creative imagery causes portions of the brain associated with visual thinking to go offline. Underusing your right brain can cause it to atrophy to a certain degree, as it will contribute less and less, and play an increasingly diminished role in your thinking. The mind is a lesser body when you are not utilizing your visual and creative modes of thought, and it will function less efficiently.

A tale of two Geniuses

Ancient methods of behaviour and contemporary systems of thought have been the object of much study, as great minds search for the secret to what makes minds better. To be sure, this continuing saga of cranial exploration is far from over.

However, functional models and methods of mind expansion have been formulated and are ready to be introduced to the breadth of present day humanity. An answer, surely not the only one, but a sound one, has been engineered to heighten the intelligence and efficiency of the brain. A promising methodology for increased human potential has been found by looking to the past.

An integration of the 2,200-year-old Socratic Method with the historically potent Einsteinian Deep Thought Experiments

"One ancient, one contemporary—separated by more than 2,000 years of history, but bound by their mental gifts, their highly efficient systems of thought and the revolutionary abilities they carried."

VTH

has given rise to a technique far beyond the scope and efficiency of those systems that have come before it—opening an easily walked path to capturing our authentic potential.

To act as a prologue, this tale of two geniuses has been written to provide you with a historical background of the Infinity Mind system—a working knowledge of the fundamental principles that underpin this new technique.

Einstein: Master of Visual Thinking

Those who employ methods of visual thinking and fully utilize their total organism do so with great reward. Many credit various techniques of visual thought with causing over 90 percent of the major scientific discoveries and technical inventions of the past few centuries. Kekule's dream, about intertwined snakes swallowing their own tails in his fireplace, taught him the structure of the benzene ring, the basis of all organic chemistry. After toiling for so long and looking for the idea he needed, Elias Howe's nightmare of cannibals surrounding him in attack, whose spears happened to have holes in their heads, provided inspiration for the sewing machine. Niccola Tesla's internal visual prophecies gave way to the electric power system, granting the world a major part of the electronics industry and changing our way of life.

Despite this confirmed historical record of successful use, visual thinking was never popularized by its users; rather, this visionary basis of discovery was concealed lest peer acceptance be shattered and credibility be lost if visualization was known to be the extricating factor in these major discoveries.

It was Albert Einstein, the father of modern science and extensive practitioner of visual thinking, who popularized this means of thinking, now known as the Einsteinian technique of Deep Thought. His mastery and unequalled ability in this style of thought assisted him in capturing a great deal of his potential intelligence and, thus, use his powerful mind to generate insights and theories that changed the world.

"Imagination is more important than knowledge."
    Albert Einstein

By initiating a running visualization and observing it closely to see what could be discovered from it, a world of original thought and ideas was tapped. His "train ride on a beam of light" taught him—and us—his theories of relativity, thus, remaking the whole of physics and revolutionizing science.

The Einsteinian Deep Thought Experiments hold great power, but are too directed to be productive for anything more then the extremes of relativity theory. Moreover, the personal discipline required is beyond the immediate reach of most people. It's been said that Einstein had an unequalled ability to concentrate, and even still, he would have had to hold a large rock in his hands while using this technique, so the loud bang of it falling on the floor would wake him up if he were to fall asleep.

Socrates: Master of Descriptive Assertion

Socrates' life is shrouded in a veil of mystery and uncertainty; so, much of what's known about the ancient Greek philosopher has no way of being proven—it can neither be confirmed nor denied. This is because Socrates wrote nothing, composed nothing, and recorded nothing. It's been said that he felt knowledge was a living, interactive thing that could neither be contained nor clearly defined through transcription. The only records of his work, doctrines, and philosophies exist in the writings of others, most notably, his great pupil Plato.

Through Plato, the world learned of Socrates' method of philosophical inquiry. This method was first coined as *elenchus*–a process of questioning people on the positions they assert and then leading them via questions to a contradiction, thus proving to them that their original assertion was wrong. The Socratic method is akin to a cross-examination for the truth. Socrates would use *elenchus* to modify one's position through questioning and conflict with opposing ideas, thereby seeking moral truth. This method induced the learner to examine his/her internal and external perceptions and to describe what he/she discovered there. It is this idea of the truth being pursued rather than discovered that characterizes the Socratic Method of inquiry and thought.

Case In Point

The first schools in Western cultural tradition were those of classical and early postclassical Greece. Those schools were not for the purpose of benefiting students—nor to propagate a particular school of thought. The main purpose of these schools was to provide a quality audience to which the leading thinkers and perceivers could describe their perceptions, and thus facilitate the further development of those perceptions.

Some of the better among these thinkers, such as the Sophists and Socrates specifically, would return the favour by drawing out their listeners in turn, either through acute questioning of one or two students at a time, or a fierce argument with perhaps a half-dozen at a time. This process became known as the Socratic Method, a methodology that has grown to define the means and techniques of modern-day education around the globe.

Historically, the practice of the classical Socratic Method was so often accompanied by such huge leaps of perception, understanding and growth that all its most noted practitioners became convinced that all knowledge and understanding are already within each learner and need merely to be "drawn forth."

Socrates was known to have never taken a position, as he radically and sceptically claimed to know nothing at all, except that he knew nothing. He also claimed to have discovered no truth, other than that he knew no truth.

In the year 399 BC, Socrates was convicted and sentenced to death for corruption of the young, but his method of inquiry continued. For the next 2,200 years, this drawing forth had such currency that education itself was named after this ancient concept: *educate* means to *draw forth*.

During the 2,200 years of Socratic education, from a population base of but a few thousand citizens, most of whom soldiered, sold olives, politicked or followed some other interests and pursuits, classical Greece (500-336 BC) produced more cultural giants and geniuses than has all of Earth's 5.5 billion people during this past half-century. Similarly, Renaissance Europe (1300-1700), with a population of a few hundred thousand citizens, radically outproduced our 5.5 billion in the production of geniuses and cultural giants. Why is this?

"I do nothing but go about persuading you all, old and young alike, not to take thought for your persons or your properties, but and chiefly to care about the greatest improvement of the soul. I tell you that virtue is not given by money, but that from virtue comes money and every other good of man, public as well as private. This is my teaching, and if this is the doctrine which corrupts the youth, I am a mischievous person."

Socrates

"Over the course of contemporary history, strategies of deep thought not only survived but exerted enormous influence on the evolution of society. Those individuals who gained access to these strategies of accelerated mental processing are responsible for virtually every great discovery and invention of our contemporary history."
                VTH

The new global economy no longer depends on the Socratic style of education, but rather on didactic teaching (instructional)—a method that has reaped poor results that can easily be observed throughout North America. The promise that is the Socratic Method has been cast aside in favour of a simpler and less effective manner of teaching. While it will be difficult for the world as a whole to switch the current mode of learning, this doesn't have to stop you.

overview

Humanity as a whole never tapped the potential these methods hold, because by themselves, the Socratic and Einsteinian systems were difficult to practice, and thus, relatively few did so. Just as any newly conceived process in its early or primitive form, they were crude and, for many, difficult to employ. These techniques of functioning caught on among the brilliant and masterful minds of our past, but not the general population.

By forming a union between the Socratic Method and the Einstein method of Deep Thought, an innovative technique has been created that is not only simply executed and used, but is superior in power and productivity. Modifications to these historically potent systems have resulted in a method that anyone can use to discover their own great answers and truths. Dr. Win Wenger, father of the fundamentals behind this brain technology, has found the technique to be so easily practiced, " . . . that out of the last few thousand people worked with, not one was unable to perform it—not one individual didn't experience an increase in their IQ." You don't have to be an Einstein to enjoy the same results as these people have. The 99.99 percent of your brain that is out of reach is now easily accessible, with no barrier as to how far ahead one can fly with this new synergistic solution to greater intelligence.

Just as mathematics suddenly became workable with the advent of the Arabic numeral system, so has mind expansion. Finally, so many centuries later, a method of harnessing the infinite powers of the mind is ready for adoption and use by all.

"FROM SOCRATES' LOOSELY ORGANIZED ASSEMBLY OF PHILOSOPHERS TO EINSTEIN'S CLOSELY KNIT COMMUNITY OF SCIENTIFIC HYPOTHESIZERS, DIFFERENT STRAINS OF ANALOGOUS STRATEGIES HAVE BEEN EMPLOYED FOR THOUSANDS OF YEARS. BUT DUE TO THE SHROUDED NATURE OF THESE GROUPS, SUCH DOCTRINES REMAINED INACCESSIBLE AND LARGELY UNTAPPED. THIS HAS NOW CHANGED."

Volition Thought House

PHASE

Infinity Mind System

KEY SUCCESS STRATEGY
engage every 24 hrs

build your iMind

The brain is an organ of equal opportunity—the entire spectrum of the populace has approximately 100 billion brain cells, tiny self-contained computers capable of processing about one million bits of information. This holds true for the world's greatest minds and the world's greatest failures. This is something you have in common with history's brightest philosophers, thinkers, geniuses, explorers, physicists, neurologists and political leaders.

"Deep within man dwell those slumbering powers; powers that would astonish him, that he never dreamed of possessing; forces that would revolutionize his life if aroused and put into action."

Orison Swett Marden

The human mind is bestowed with an incredible amount of neurons, but it isn't the magnitude of this physiological fact that is of greatest importance; rather it is the quantity of connections that are made between those neurons that dictates the operational qualities of the mind. Each neuron holds the potential to grow up to 20,000 connecting branches, or dendrites, so it's the greatest percentage capture of this potential that transfers into a mind of pinnacle quality and high intelligence.

But the only way these connections or dendrites can be formed is through exercising and developing the brain.

Research shows that, if you don't exercise and maintain your neurons and dendrites, your brain will become just as weak and flabby as your abdominals can become without training. Superachievers exercise not only their physical system, but their system of thought as well. The Infinity Mind System is the prescribed training system for the human mind—your guide to the strengthening of your brain.

The concept of intelligence has only been in existence for the last 100 years, but it has already undergone substantial change, as it is no longer a static or fixed quantity, but an entity of dynamic proportions. Intelligence is not handed out at birth, but earned over a lifetime. Craft your infinite mind and capture the intelligence of which you are truly capable. Tap your limitless potential and make it available for use. Powered by your internal engine of creativity, let the Infinity Mind System guide you in the creation of your iMind. In the words of Rene Descartes, "It is not enough to have a good mind; the main thing is to use it well." Be one of the forerunners of the new frontier—forge an influential mind and become a leader of tomorrow.

"The empires of the future are the empires of the mind."
Sir Winston Churchill

Progression Key

This is the Infinity Mind System— it is meant to be executed in its entirety by following the chronological steps of described action. Let each session run from 10 to 30 minutes.

This system will bring you great change. By accumulating at least 30 hours (10-30 minutes at a time) of true IMS application as directed herein, you will gain at least 20 IQ points and most likely many more. Your vocabulary will jump noticeably and your intuitive gains will be even more striking. Execute the

Infinity Mind System as outlined below, and in time, you will become an intellectual giant.

take action to capture your Intellect: The fundamental workings of this program have been tested by Southwest State University since 1989, found to increase your IQ by 20 points after 25 hours of execution: that's 4/5 of an IQ point gain per hour of practice.

Step 1
enter the state

The wide spectrum of brain activity falls into four different levels of intensity. Just as our muscular system operates at peak exertion during athletics and at a relaxed pace while sleeping, our brain operates at different levels of wave intensity— racing with incredible force and our neurons bursting into action during a high-stimulus situation, or slowly purring in deep REM sleep.

Beta: 13 - 40 HZ Brain Waves/Second (Normal Awake State)
Descriptors: ATTENTIVE, CONSCIOUS, NARROW FOCUS
You are awake, attentive and alert. Your mind is sharp and focused. It makes connections quickly and easily, as you're primed to do work that requires your full attention. In the Beta state, neurons fire in great number and in rapid succession, helping you achieve heightened performance—but barring you from flashes of intuition. The Beta state is best for

tackling intense scientific information and making the initial effort to understand something.

Alpha: 7 - 12 Brain Waves/Second (Ideal State for Learning)

Descriptors: VISUALIZATION, RELAXATION, INGENUITY

Your brain activity slows from the brisk patterns of Beta into the more mellow waves of Alpha. In the Alpha state, you are truly relaxed and your awareness expands. A creative energy begins to surface. New ideas and solutions to problems flash like lightning into your mind. Fears vanish. A liberating sense of peace and wellbeing is experienced.

When Alpha brain waves become more dominant, logical left-brain activity—which normally acts as a filter or censor to the subconscious—drops its guard. This allows the more intuitive, emotional and creative depths of the mind that exist just below the threshold of consciousness to become increasingly influential.

Theta: 4 - 7 Brain Waves/Second (mysterious state of intuition)

Descriptors: INTUITION, MEMORY, DEEP THOUGHT

As your brain slows, you fall into a subtle and mysterious Theta state of deeper relaxation, where your mind slows almost to the point of sleep. Theta is the brain state where the unexplainable occurs in the wake of your own neurological activity. Theta brings forward flickers of dreamlike imagery, heightened receptivity, early memories and surges of inspiration. Theta can bring you deep states of meditation, where you experience a sensation of suspension or floating. As Theta is an expansive state, you may feel your mind expand beyond the boundaries of your body and enter the energy fields that circulate around your physical self.

Delta: 0 - 4 Brain Waves/Second (State of Deep Sleep)

Descriptors: DETACHED AWARENESS, SLEEPING,

The slowest of all brain wave frequencies, Delta brain waves are long, deep and undulating, most commonly associated with deep dreamless sleep.

Your deep Delta state of brain wave activity is one of harmonious relaxation, where both sides of the brain work in synchronization. Psychologists have found that this heightened state of relaxation opens up the right lobe of your brain and grants you greater access to your subconscious memory, which makes this state ideal for working with mental imagery and optimal for learning and capturing information. Call upon your Delta state to ignite your creative energies and bring into action the infinite resources of your mind.

It's integral that you quickly and efficiently channel your state of mind into its accelerative state of melodic functioning—to resynchronize your mental and physical processes, and prime your brain for expansion. The following exercise will power-assist you to achieve this Alpha state of mind.

Rhythmic Relaxation
1

Select a place where you can be alone and allow yourself to relax completely. A library or any other quiet public place may not be the best choice due to the presence of others; you may

"Solitude is as needful to the imagination as society is wholesome for the character."

James Russell Lowell

feel self-conscious, this may cause harm to your concentration.

Places such as your office, bedroom or living room (if your residence is empty) are good places when you are just beginning. Once you begin to feel comfortable and increase your skill with the IMS, you can begin to use the IMS in more contentious places such as an airplane, library, bus, a quiet common area, etc. When you finish an IMS session and you find others peering at you in a curiously strange manner, make a light joke: "Meditate once a day to keep the doctor away." As long as you can enjoy a certain degree of tranquility, you can get comfortable, and the place doesn't matter once you've mastered the IMS.

"Minds are like parachutes; they work best when open."
Lord Thomas Dewar

2

Allow your body to relax totally and release the tension flowing within your muscles. Close your eyes and, breathing through your nose, inhale as much air as you can for a four-second time period. Then hold this air in your lungs for four seconds. Finally, exhale over a four-second time period and feel the deep sense of relaxation. Continue to do this three times and then continue on in six-second intervals.

Breathe in six seconds / hold six seconds / breathe out six seconds.
Repeat four times

Breathe in eight seconds / hold eight seconds / breathe out eight seconds.
Repeat four times.

Breathe deeply, letting stress and anxiety flow out and harmony flow in with every breath. Feel the wave of relaxation overcome your physical body and flow from your head to your toe. You should feel a certain heaviness and warmth to your body; this indicates that your blood vessels have relaxed and dilated. Such an experience of warmth influences your entire circulatory system, as the relaxation of your blood vessels will spread from your appendages to the coronary vessels. This results in a definite shifting of your body experience and induces results that are far superior to those of conventional relaxation techniques. At this point, your brain waves will have slowed to a leisurely seven to 12 cycles per second—the Alpha state. You are now ready to focus on the given task.

Be careful not to fall asleep, as the human body closely associates the deep Alpha state with resting. This process will become easier as you gain a talent for attaining the Alpha state. Soon you will learn to recognize what it feels like to enter the state and you will speed through this process in a matter of a few breaths.

Step 2
execute with intention and belief

Declare your goal of the moment. Avow your present purpose and create a sense of intention within your mind. Doing so will form an extraordinary attractor that will trigger the complexities of your mind, causing your brain's reflexive sorter to take your intention and align its vast resources to meet that intention, thereby igniting effective action. This internal attractor phenomenon will only work if you believe the desired outcome to be attainable and if you believe that you can

"Great spirits have always found violent opposition from mediocre minds. The latter cannot understand it when a man does not thoughtlessly submit to hereditary prejudices but honestly and courageously uses his intelligence."

Albert Einstein

increase your IQ and capture more of your brain's power. The goal of greater intelligence that the IMS is designed to create, must exist within your belief system—only then will the IMS redefine your abilities.

When undertaking a grand task such as this, you must act in accordance with the Belief Maxim: "Whatever you believe with feeling and conviction becomes your reality." You know the power this maxim commands—you know it has jurisdiction over your whole existence. Let's make it work for you.

mind conditioning

The strategy you are about to put to use will revolutionize your mind's faculties and increase your IQ. If you haven't developed a firm trust in this statement or you simply feel unequipped to master this technique, and you do nothing about it, then you have already lost. Your efforts will be compromised and its effectiveness sabotaged. If your feelings towards the IMS are those of skepticism, then it will take action to change this.

Before continuing through the IMS process, refer to Phase 1.2: Mind Conditioning to rid yourself of doubt and inject success-minded belief into your subconscious. One Mind Conditioning session won't rid you of skepticism, but over time this barrier can be broken down by taking daily progressive action. The more time you take to condition your mind to act efficiently, the more it will begin to do so. Program the following affirmation into your subconscious, so as to maximize your performance:

"I have the ability to master the Infinity Mind System and

activate my untapped genius."

Once you've charged this affirmation into your subconscious, try to think of additional affirmations that suit you and your thoughts perfectly, statements that strengthen your belief that you can expand your mind, as well as statements that counter any negative thoughts you may hold about the effectiveness of the IMS. Perhaps phrases such as those to the right suit your present thoughts well and may help you execute with greater confidence.

I can capture my total intelligence.

step 3
visualize and emotionalize realization

Now close your eyes and clearly visualize your intellectual quotient (IQ) rising, just as the red liquid in a thermometer would slowly rise on a hot summer day. Make a picture in your mind of yourself thinking in a more decisive and fluid manner, seeing every variable and analyzing every fact. See yourself debating issues with control, anticipating the other person's point well before they actually reveal it and guiding discussion with tactician. See in your mind's eye a *you* with an extensive vocabulary, stunning memory, a grand sense of humour and heightened spatial awareness. Imagine yourself as a successful person who has learned to operate with greater efficiency and mental faculty, achieving your goals and acting effectively.

This proven technique will give me access to my greater abilities.

I am human and so just as any other human, I have far greater ability than I am presently using or detecting.

Use all of your senses: seeing, hearing, smelling, tasting and touching to intuitively feel the various elements of your success-filled destiny—put yourself inside the picture you've created. Feel the pleasure and elation that will come with mastering your mind and working at a greater level of functioning.

step 4
conceive an image

With your eyes still closed, make certain your eyes have adjusted to the lack of light and have adapted to the darkness. Peer deep into the shadows, with your mind open, become aware of what your mind is naturally creating. Try to detect what lies in front of you. What may first appear is a subtle wave of greyscale shapes, gesticulating movement or flashes of random colour. Concentrate on whatever you see and watch for the development of a vivid mental image. At any moment and at every moment, there exists an image within your mind's eye—a visual entity of your own creation. It is there, but you must first sense its existence. This is the most important step in the process, if not properly executed, can bar you from grasping a greater hold on your intellectual abilities.

"I am imagination. I can see what the eyes cannot see. I can hear what the ears cannot hear. I can feel what the heart cannot feel."
Peter Nivio Zarlenga

By simply closing your eyes and observing, more than half of the population will see an image instantaneously—a dart board hanging from a wall, a ball bouncing down the street, a pouncing cat, a soaring bird. With focus and some effort, you'll find a strong, clear, definite image or set of images; at first, some may simply see just a glimpse—a faint impression which you might think is hardly worth describing. When you first start using this process, you may be uncertain as to whether you are making up the idea rather than really seeing an image. Throw this slice of skepticism out the window and trust your senses. With practice there won't be any doubt in your mind as to the validity of what you're seeing. Remember, try to sense and detect what's in your mind's eye now, not what you decide to see there.

The human mind has stunning and majestic imaginative powers. Allow these powers to take control and send you surging through a wormhole of ingenious creativity. The more shock you feel over what you see there, the more you are engaging your offline senses—the more potent and far-reaching resources of the brain that are far beyond your conscious realm of thought.

Troubleshooting:

It has been proven that not all individuals have been able to properly execute this step in the process—sense an image. If you have trouble doing so, the following alternative image trigger techniques will get you on the right track.

-With your eyes closed, reach for the imaginary door that is in front of you and fling it open to reveal what exists on the other side. Feel/smell/taste/hear what is there. Begin to describe it. If you like, you can substitute curtains on a window for the door, the lid to a treasure chest, the door to a closet, the trap door in a mansion or anything else you can think of.

-Look up at the light on your ceiling for 20 seconds (not a blindingly bright light) and then close your eyes. Begin to describe the image that forms on your eyelids, watch how it develops into something else.

-A meal is set before you. What does it look like, taste like, feel like, sound like? Describe it, allow your image to develop and stream into something else.

"When I examine myself and my methods of thought, I come to the conclusion that the gift of fantasy has meant more to me than my talent for absorbing positive knowledge."
Albert Einstein

-You are in an airplane, you jump out, parachute down into a foreign land. What do you see as you approach the earth and where do you land? How does it feel, sound, smell and look?

-Go into a closet or bathroom and, with your eyes shut, quickly turn the light on and off several times. Describe the vivid and powerful colours, shapes and patterns that dance across your eyelids.

"The engine of the IMS is Step 5; this action elicits an almost paranormal response from the human mind—the leaps and bounds in functioning it stimulates is astounding."
VTH

-Open the cover of a book and describe what you sense, feel, see and experience. This means of creating an image will be useful for the coming phase.

See where these starting points take you. Allow the images to flow away from the beginning image and look for the subtleties that come forth.

step 5
describe and develop your image

An image exists within your mind's eye and you've latched onto its existence. It's now time for you to start your tape recorder (if you don't have a live listener) and verbally describe the image aloud in as much detail and with as much speed as possible.

The dormant parts of your brain that the Infinity Mind System is intended to bring online work with sensory visuals and images, even in matters of logic. If you merely explain your image: "I see a mountain," you aren't utilizing your heightened senses and ingenious perceptions. Detail every element, aspect and feature of your image. Describe your image and the scene you see with vivacity and energy, as a painter would describe a rich and masterful piece of canvas. Only then will you engage the Socratic effect and achieve the leaps in perception that are possible.

"I'm gazing at a continuous ebb and flow of mountain peaks and valleys. I seem to be standing at the edge of a cliff, the wind is surging through my hair, the smell of evergreens is running through my nose, rigid and solid plates of rock are holding me in place, with granules of stone and dust crunching beneath my feet—brown, grey and black in colour. In the distance is an eagle . . . "

Swiftly describe your image. Don't grasp for words or think of ways to describe it; rather, quickly and verbally project outwards the initial words that flow forth. The more practice you have, the greater the descriptive ability you will have and the greater the descriptive vocabulary you will command. A vivid narrative may feel difficult at first, but this will quickly pass. At times, you may feel that you're forcing a description out and overly describing your image to the point of making some up. This is perfectly natural and is completely all right, as it will only cause more detail to come to your attention.

Don't let your internal judge or critic hold you back from saying something; simply disengage this natural inclination to censor what it is you say and never think twice as to whether or not something is worth mentioning—flow forth with your description, never halting. Follow the statement: "If it occurs to you, express it!" A rapid and continuous descriptive gush creates what Win Wenger calls an almost venturi force, or suction action, pulling other perceptions into focus. Describing your image in a quick manner will cause you to be surprised at how much more detail will come to your attention, even if you feel your image is already clear. By removing all conscious direction of image description so that your imagined experience can come forth clean and uninterrupted, you will begin to activate the dormant regions of your mind.

The Necessity of an Audience

The key to activating the force of this exercise requires that you utilize a live listener or a potential listener represented by a tape recorder. Without a listener and external focus, the procedure does very little for you. A world-class pianist will never play their best without an audience for whom to perform—a pop star will always lack punch and energy during a sound check and a professional soccer player will always run a little slower and perform at less than what he's capable of in practice. An audience elicits a different level of performance from you. It creates an intention to meet—a goal of describing your image in so much depth and detail that the listener gets to see exactly what you are seeing. Without a listener, or potential listener (tape recorder), you will tend to lighten your descriptions, ease your analysis of your image and not outwardly voice that which you would otherwise. Without an audience, you have no one for whom to perform.

This same dynamic of human behaviour comes into play when in conversation. If you are sitting in a coffee shop and speaking with a friend, the dialogue would be very external—you would verbally communicate your thoughts in an external manner by talking. If you were sitting in a coffee shop without a friend and felt compelled to enter a conversation with yourself (this isn't advised, unless you really want to put on a show), then some of the dialogue would occur only in your head—you wouldn't need to describe verbally all that you are thinking about because there is no second party. You would naturally hold back much of what you would otherwise say.

Outwardly verbalizing your description causes you to enter a new plane of analysis. You need to choose verbs, adjectives and descriptors to explain what you are seeing. And as you are thinking of how to express what you are seeing in your mind, you will naturally think of different ways of describing it. Perhaps a few different analogies and metaphors come to mind and as you *over* describe your image in such ways, more details and features of the image will become apparent. Always be alert to new-found areas of detail and newly discovered aspects of your image—describe such new impressions as they come. The greater the depth to which you dive, the more symbolic the meaning and emblematic the commentary you will find.

Cinema for One

It is like operating your own private movie screening, only in a theater of the mind. When you close your eyes, it is like sitting down in an empty dark theatre. When you create an image in your mind, it is like turning on the projector in your own personal cinema. With your eyelids as the screen, your subconscious as the projectionist and your conscious mind the viewer, the IMS manufactures the most dynamic imagery possible. And just as watching movies is an entertaining and enjoyable experience, so is the IMS. The things your subconscious mind projects onto your eyelids are often mesmerizing, compelling and thrilling.

All this is done most easily with eyes shut, so that your inner visual circuits aren't distracted away from these initially subtler signals and so they can operate at full sensitivity. In other words, please keep your eyes closed during such processing, in order to see more freely.

At times you may feel as though you're grasping for more to describe and searching for more detail. You may feel as though you've discovered the deep profundity of your image, have described it fully and are grasping for more. This may happen quite often in the learning stages. The solution to this is simple.

"We must walk con- sciously only part way toward our goal and then leap in the dark to our success."
Henry David Thoreau

Fight through these gaps and fill them with a description. Continue to discover and develop your image, even if you are taking some extra liberties and are making some up. As your skill grows, this will soon come to pass. Remember, even seemingly trivial impressions or simple images should be described in such richly textured detail as to force anyone listening to experience and see what you are describing.

Invent a Solution

The IMS will draw forth inventive solutions and creative answers, enlighten you about yourself and your external world and inspire clever strokes of brilliance that you may not even be looking for. As you grow to harness your intellectual abilities, the IQ-increasing benefits of the IMS will grow less and less valuable; it is the ingenious ideas and solutions that it can provide that will become the true reward of the process.

This advanced use of the IMS will draw forth ideas of ingenuity and innovation from your subconscious, much like a source of light draws insects at dusk. Entering the Alpha state and thus opening your subconscious resources to your sidebands of thought, transports you to a unique state of reception—causing you to pick up and receive messages of eminence from your mind, much like a satellite dish picks up radio waves and open air broadcasts from the atmosphere.

The IMS draws from your richer, image-driven resources of the brain and thus the grandest of ideas, answers and solutions come forth as visual representations. Ideas that come forth as words are often from the surface, bubbling up from our verbal consciousness—a source of limited ingeniuity and creativity.

It is in your subconscious that you will find that million-dollar idea, that perfect solution and that otherwise unthinkable thought. Like a timeless encyclopedia of knowledge, your mind will always supply an answer, if only you hear what it says.

"Problems cannot be solved at the same level of awareness that created them."
Albert Einstein

Case In Point

In 1840, American inventor Elias Howe went to sleep plagued by his financial difficulties. That night he had a nightmare in which cannibals surrounded him, jabbing at him with sharp-pointed spears. He fought them valiantly, but to no avail. Just as the end was near, Howe noticed that each of the cannibals' spears had a hole at its point.

At that instant, Elias Howe awoke from his sleep, his mind still flooded with the images of those pierced spear points. Immediately, Howe realized that his dream had supplied him with an idea for designing a needle that would vastly improve the crude sewing machines of his day. Howe went to work on the idea and before long, he had invented the sewing machine needle we now use today. Is the latest invention residing in your subconscious?

To formulate an answer to a problem, ask a question of your mind during Step 2, so as to align your subconscious resources to meet that end. The question can be stated in a very specific manner: "Infinite mind, I would like to know how I should design the graphical interface for this project," or in a very general manner, "Infinite mind, this is a question I would like to answer." Proceed your way through the IMS and your solution will be presented. Many other problem solving systems spend a large amount of time redefining the question and analyzing the problem. This is not the case when using the IMS because the subconscious mind knows the problem or question of paramount importance and immediately begins processing a solution. During Einstein's deep thought experiments, he was often unclear as to the exact problem he was trying to solve, but his subconscious new exactly and so a solution was always generated.

"All that it takes is an idea that is 10% new to make 10 million dollars."

Decode the Solution

If it is a solution to a question you wish to find, there are certain things you can do to help this along. When you are developing your image as described in Step 5—immersed in the visual world you've conceived—latch onto a specific element of the image; a central object in what you see, whether it be a tractor, box, or door. While searching through your image, approach the object and reach out to touch it; study its feel by describing it aloud. You can try to ask the object for more information: "How do you fit in as part of my solution?" or "Why are you here?" Look for any reaction or change in the image as a result of your question and describe any changes you see. Interact with and speak to the object in your imagery to get to know that object in an increased capacity. It exists in your mind's eye because it represents a solution to your question—it holds a significant meaning to the answer you are searching for, so draw out clues to help determine the symbolic meaning of it.

If you've used the IMS for 10 to 15 minutes to find a solution and are having a difficult time deciphering the meaning of your images, ask this question of your mind: "Subconscious, please show me a new symbolic representation of the solution you are trying to tell me." Go through the IMS again and you will receive a new set of visual pictures that represent the same solution. When you are finished, begin to compare the two sets of images and look for similarities. Once you've determined the consistencies (colour, shape, context, texture, feel), you can pinpoint the key themes and then have greater success at deciphering the answer under the surface that is trying to break through.

> *"The best way to get a good idea is to get a lot of ideas."*
> Linus Pauling, two-time Nobel Laureate

If you are still having difficulty seeing the solution, summarize the running images you visualized and recap your experience by verbally describing them aloud. Perhaps you could draw out a mind map and create a graphical mapping of your images. The symbolism should quickly become obvious as you look upon the visual pictures with a reflective perspective. At a certain point you will come to master the IMS to such a degree that the answers to your questions will be brought forth in mere minutes, every time.

AFTER 12 HOURS OF USING THE INFINITY MIND SYSTEM, YOU WILL HAVE INCREASED YOUR IQ BY 9.6 POINTS AND STIMULATED GREATER VISUAL INTELLIGENCE AND SPATIAL ABILITY.

INCORPORATE THE IMS INTO YOUR FUTURE AND LET YOUR INTELLECTUAL PERFORMANCE AND CREATIVITY CONTINUE TO IMPROVE IN AN INFINITE CAPACITY.

phase shift

Phase Three

Imagine standing on a beach, only, unlike any other beach, when you look outward you see the entire world before you, in place of the ocean. You see people interacting and loving, playing and learning, as well as those who look tired, distressed and unhappy. You see businesses booming and others fading, working professionals being promoted while others are demoted, students succeeding while others are failing. As you watch the flow of money, capital, cars, homes and toys you begin to notice a strong concentration of these assets around those who are achieving. You observe this pattern of dynamics and see a distinct and separate factor that determines where all others fall into place . . . information. As you watch the steady and even stream of data, you see it bypass the unhappy and flow to the happy. You watch it being absorbed by successful minds and run off and down the side of mediocre minds. You come to a sudden realization; it's information that drives success, as with it comes knowledge, a tool with which assets are amassed, happiness is crafted, victory is created, and legacies are built.

IN THE PAGES THAT FOLLOW, YOU WILL GAIN WAYS TO BYPASS THE LIMITED PROCESSING CAPABILITIES OF YOUR CONSCIOUS MIND AND CONNECT WITH THE EXPANDED PROCESSING CAPABILITIES OF YOUR SUBCONSCIOUS—THE PLACE WHERE KNOWLEDGE IS CREATED.

Use Phase 3 to stop the information run-off:

INJECT THE INFORMATION OF THE UNIVERSE INTO YOUR MIND AND HARNESS THE POWERS IT GRANTS.

Learn to capitalize on the invisible advantage that information represents and let the intangibles of wisdom and knowledge drive your performance.

PROGRESSION SCHEDULE

Day seven Study
    3.1 Infinity Reading System Introduction

Day eight Study
    3.2 Preview Infinity Reading System

Day nine Action
    3.2 Use the Infinity Reading System

IRS Introduction

The Knowledge Economy

Over the course of history, the human race has progressed through countless stages. Initially, there was the prehistoric age where the human race merely came to terms with its environment. Our species lived in caves and struggled to survive in a very hostile environment. Then there was the progression towards control of the environment and the formation of social constructs—leading to the rise and fall of great civilizations such as the Roman and Greek. As time passed, we experienced the Agricultural Age, the Industrial Age and so forth until we entered the present, the Information Age. For the last two hundred years, neo-classical economics has recognized only two factors of production: labour and capital. This is no longer the case, as information and knowledge have become the primary wealth-creating assets, just as the latter two replaced land and labor 200 years before.

"Information is the only true asset in the new economy."
VTH

We're now an information society in an economy driven by knowledge, the generation and exploitation of which play the predominant part in the creation of wealth and macroeconomic growth. It is knowledge that comprises today's basic form of capital; it is the lifeblood that binds the present and future of our global society; and it is the currency of our modern times, delineating our age from those of our ancestors. As organisms of cognition, information forms the content of our conscious thought and that of our subconscious database.

"The stealth and skill with which one absorbs information, is the only long-term determinant of success."
VTH

We see the external world through the filtered eyes that information artificially creates and sense only what that information allows. Information tells how to feel and think. The words happy, sad, sick, excited and depressed exist, so we often feel these ways. Information from the external world directs our beliefs and values; if we receive information that convinces us we are incapable, then that is what we believe. If information from the outside world supports the respect of those with gorgeous homes and fast cars, then this is what we will respect and value. It's what separates geniuses from laborers, winners from losers, heads of state from victims of the state. Information is the true cloth of our existence; it is the formative structure of our world and it defines all that is.

Cutting-edge technologies have increased the mobility of information to such a point that knowledge and expertise can be transported instantaneously around the world. A well-calculated gain in process efficiency, technology or product quality by one company can be eliminated by aggressive improvements by a global competitor overnight.

The company that thrives in the knowledge economy breathes in information and breathes out innovation. The only comparative advantage a company can enjoy is their ability to combine market and technology know-how with the creative talents of knowledge workers to solve a constant stream of competitive problems—their ability to derive innovative value from information. Countries and companies that thrive in the knowledge economy launch strategic education plans, not to force information upon their people, but to teach them how to learn, for only then can an organization truly mine the globe's knowledge sources and fully capitalize on the abundance of information.

"Information is the input and wealth is the finished product."
VTH

Those who wield information as a weapon of competition are the real contenders in the knowledge economy. Energy, industrial power, natural resources and corporate might are no longer the means of the unassailable monopolist—with one fell swoop, knowledge and information can power a new challenger to the top and topple even the biggest of institutions.

"The brighter you are, the more you have to learn."
Don Herold

The entrepreneur who reaps growing profits and enjoys titanic fortunes learns at a furious pace, always remembering that it's the rapid speed with which he/she digests information that accounts for his/her success and prevents his/her extinction.

Case In Point

In today's digital world, the brief life cycle of information results in information being of incredible value today and no longer so in 48 months or 48 minutes. Those who ride these surging waves of data—the true mavericks of the new economy—seize the opportunities found in this raging ocean of wealth and rise to the forefront of their respective industries. The sluggish and bloated of Wall Street will begin to falter and stumble as their inefficient use of knowledge catches up to them—complacency brings no reward. A paradigm shift is soon to occur as more and more people recognize this opportunity. Join this new wave of potential and take possession of that of which you are capable.

"Knowledge is the life-blood of the new economy and those who don't tap into this flowing reservoir will fall victim to mediocrity."
VTH

The Lifelong Quest of Learning

"What we become depends on what we read after all of the professors have finished with us. The greatest university of all is a collection of books."

Thomas Carlyle

"I have often reflected upon the new vistas that reading opened to me. I knew right there in prison that reading had changed forever the course of my life. As I see it today, the ability to read awoke in me some long dormant craving to be mentally alive."

Malcolm X

Learning is a continuous process—one that should never cease. Everything you are and everything you are to become is a result of what you learn. It constitutes the abilities you possess, the knowledge you exercise and the force for success you have. It has been said that the person who graduates today and stops learning tomorrow faces a slow decline in their ability and intellect. You can commit no surer a mistake than to stop learning, for the future you will soon confront is one you'd rather not face. To stop gaining knowledge is in effect slamming the brakes on your own personal evolution.

Personal development and self-expansion by way of learning is certainly not compulsory—but neither is survival. Every human being has an equal choice over both, but the fact is over 90 percent of the general population choose not to continue learning and .0001 percent choose not to survive. They fail to realize that the true fruits of life are internal. It is through the mind that one experiences the world and when it is closed, one ceases to live.

In the words of Ralph Waldo Emerson, brilliant writer and lecturer, "What is the hardest task in the world? To think." If the average man was faced with two choices; the first, to be a labourer and the second, to be a great thinker, he would almost always pick the second. But why then, in actuality, does the average man do the first? Because thinking and learning are tasks reserved for those with determination, desire, courage and the deep-down hunger for personal growth. Learning is an undertaking that requires a long-term investment and is one that pays long-term dividends. The average person acts only in the short-term, always looking for immediate gratification and the instant pleasures.

A great man once said that learning how to learn in a maximum capacity is life's most important skill. The person who figures out how to harness the collective genius of his or her faculties is going to blow the competition away.

As you've discovered by now, the subconscious is our largely untapped and offline expanse of the brain. Scientific inquiry hasn't even begun to comprehend the full power and ability that lies there—but what we can be sure of is that there are no known boundaries to the ability of the mind; it is truly a limitless resource with an infinite amount of potential. Every experience, encounter, incident, note, message, sentence, paragraph, page, or book your mind lays witness to becomes locked within it. If one can't remember the thing they read in the morning's newspaper or the book they read five years ago, it's not because they don't know it. It is the process of recall that is at fault, for everything is permanently engrained in our memory, in our subconscious.

The human mind is truly a database of infinite proportions, yet this resource goes undetected by most individuals, because the majority of conscious thought and perception occur in the regions of the brain that support verbal communication, causing our conscious mind to work at the pace of verbal communication, which is usually one word at a time. It is within functional realms of the brain that aren't linked to verbal communication where astonishing feats are accomplished. Electroprobe measurements show the performance levels in such expanses of the brain to be 10,000 to 100 million times

"There is no expedient to which a man will not go to avoid the real labor of thinking."
Thomas Edison

"Learning is not attained by chance. It must be sought for with ardour and attended to with diligence."
Abigail Adams, First Lady and Presidential Mother

"One hundred and eighteen of the 400 individuals on Forbes richest list, never even finished college. They were self-taught and discovered their own powerful force for success."
VTH

faster.

Research in Point

A wide body of minds from both science and psychology backgrounds have hypothesized that the conscious mind only absorbs seven (plus or minus two) chunks of information at once; using the conscious mind as your access point for information absorption creates a tremendous restriction. To absorb a truly infinite amount of information, keep your conscious mind out of the way and utilize the infinite capacity for learning that exists underneath your conscious surface.

"It is the only example of evolution providing a species with an organ which it does not know how to use; a luxury organ, which will take its owner thousands of years to learn to put to proper use—if it ever does."
Arthur Koestler

Imagine scanning the internet with a cutting-edge, Intel, processor-driven desktop computer with only a 12.8 kb modem. When accessing the internet, you are forced to wait as your computer slowly receives the packets of data, slowly pieces together the html code and little by little displays the web page on the monitor. Then you want to click on a hyperlink to see a new page and so the process of waiting occurs all over again. Where is the problem? The computer is working at a mere percentage of its capacity, as the archaic modem downloads information at an unacceptable pace. The computer's performance is compromised, as the bottlenecks in the system cause great inefficiencies.

The same holds true for your mind. By using your conscious resources to read and absorb information, you are employing a largely inefficient channel of data input, causing you to use a mere percentage of the performance powers you contain. What a mere fraction of the population has recognized is the built-in broadband access point that each and every human has. Research on subconscious processing and unconscious perception has shown that our subconscious mind can absorb visual information through a direct access line that effectively bypasses the conscious mind. Through this access point, our brains can absorb visual text on a subliminal level, meaning, information can enter our mind below the threshold of conscious perception. Without even noticing or realizing that it's happening, textual information can be propelled into our subconscious via this information superhighway at a rate unequalled through any other means. This access point, when used, will unlock those currently unused performance powers and stop the stalling of your internal system to which you are presently accustomed.

As you enter the modern-day jungle—the new knowledge economy—it becomes readily apparent that you are no longer in a forgiving environment. There are no second chances and you are only as good as your performance. Becoming an efficient learner is not only important; it's imperative if you plan on rising up and seizing the position you know you are capable of achieving.

The great thinkers, seasoned learners and astounding intellects in every field and industry are able to think with peak speed, accuracy and logic. They have learned the best ways to acquire and retain information. *You* too can learn how to gain wisdom and absorb knowledge with a real plan of attack; learn through your direct access point to the infinite mind.

"Any sufficiently advanced technology is indistinguishable from magic."
Arthur C. Clarke

"Genius without education is like silver in the mine." It might as well not even exist, because without digging deep within that precious resource, it is completely useless."
Benjamin Franklin

"Today a reader, tomorrow a leader."
W. Fusselman

THE ABILITY TO LEARN *TAE KWON DO* IN A MATTER OF SECONDS, VIA SOFTWARE DOWNLOAD THROUGH A GLASS FIBER OPTIC CABLE INSERTED DIRECTLY INTO THE BRAIN STEM, IS NOT YET POSSIBLE—BUT NOT UNLIKE THE WORLD OF "THE MATRIX," THE THINGS YOU CAN ACCOMPLISH ONCE YOU'VE TAPPED YOUR INNER WORLD OF COGNITION WILL AMAZE YOU.

3.2
PHASE

Infinity Reading System

KEY SUCCESS STRATEGY
engage every 24 hrs

Read at the speed of sight

Engineered to give you the ability to read with full engage-
ment of your subconscious powers, the Infinity Reading
System will show you how to incorporate your industrial-
strength, infinite mental resources into your reading efforts.
To iRead isn't to simply read with greater speed, rather, to
iRead means to involve the infinite potentialities of the mind
in such a way as to inhale information and exhale wisdom,
ingenuity and genius with unimaginable force.

Superachievers dive into information with a methodical
approach. Our society has entered the era of engineered
medicinal solutions, tested and manufactured remedies and
artificial-life-supporting instruments—just as science no longer
relies on half-truths, fallacies and cultural myths, winners in
the new economy no longer rely on dated and inefficient
means of sifting through information. Like a physicist who
splits atoms, they approach a book in a surgically precise and
fastidious manner.

There is nothing instinctual about the perfect golf swing; it
is a highly mechanized and harmonious movement, incorpo-

rating every part of the body in a precisely engineered burst of effort. iReading is no different. Aside from opening one's eyes and breathing during the process, there is absolutely nothing instinctual about it. Those who have mastered the informational matrix we live in do so with a deliberate and calculated program of reading.

"The man who does not read good books has no advantage over the man who can't read them."

Mark Twain

Information is the oil of the knowledge economy. Mine this vast resource by capturing data with strategy and gaining knowledge with tactics. The IRS is your own program of information capture and with it you will become a leader in the knowledge era, much like the oil tycoons did in the industrial era. Learn to iRead and let the information flow through your veins, power your consciousness, guide your decisions and elevate your status to that of a modern day hero.

Progression Key

"Books are the legacies that a great genius leaves to mankind, which are delivered down from generation to generation as presents to the posterity of those who are yet un-born."

Joseph Addison

To iRead isn't like conventional reading at all—forget all your preconceptions about the process of reading, the manner in which it's done and how fast one can do it. Using this system will allow you to read a book that previously took eight hours, in one-tenth the time, with proficient comprehension and incredible accuracy. Using this strategy for only a short period of time will give you the ability to amass the greatest mental library the world has ever known.

You will have the learning skills to enter any domain of specialization within weeks, become current on any issue within days, ingest an entire year's worth of school homework in hours and be ahead of the game in any area of business operation in minutes. If you have the drive, no book will go unread; no story, tale or theory will be foreign to you for long, if you have the initiative to make a genius existence your reality. Those who exist at the pinnacle of reading skill can literally zoom through approximately 25,000 words per minute. The following technique has been constructed to demonstrate how you can join this skilled group of readers.

Before you begin the IRS, you must commit to one thing— you will strive to learn the system of iReading with desire, intent for self-improvement and total commitment. Make it a personal goal. You've learned how important it is to absorb information in the knowledge economy, so follow through with this in mind and use it to fuel your actions.

PROCESS ONE: CAPTURE THE INFORMATION
The Infinity Reading System begins by preparing the capsule of information, calibrating your mind for information upload and then uploading the information into your subconscious mind via iReading.

1.1
Prepare the Vessel of Information

To begin the process, one should prepare the vessel of information that will be explored, whether it be a magazine, trade journal, book, text, website or microfilm. The IRS instructions are tailored to the iReading of a book or *physical* reading material of any type; however, the process can be adopted for iReading anything.

In this case you will be uploading the information contained in a book, so in preparation one must adjust the spine so as to see both pages of the book. Just as a computer screen is flat and seamless, with no interruptions or interferences with what is being displayed, you need to prime the book until it's a smooth and flat surface of information, with the pages on an equal plane and the centre crease firmly pressed.

Do this by opening the book and laying it, with the spine down, on a table or desk top. Hold the pages upright, with the cover of the book and the spine lying flat on the table. Starting at the front of the book take about 20 pages at a time and lay them down flat. Run your fingers gently, but firmly, along the inner edge of the book simultaneously. Be firm, but gentle enough not to break the glue at the spine. Start with just the first 20 pages and slowly work your way inward, until you are at the centre of the book. With the book properly broken in, it is ready to be iRead.

This preparatory step not only achieves the obvious task of making the book more functional, but it initiates the process of iReading. As you flatten the pages and work your way towards the centre of the book, you are exposing a large portion of the pages to your brain. This will give you a greater idea of that which is contained within its pages, bringing you to think about the opportunity for growth the book represents. Begin to think about the information this book has stored away and how it can further advance your knowledge and ability.

1.2
Enter the State

At this time, you've learned the power of focus and higher functioning that the Alpha state of mind activates. Just as you did in the IMS, it is imperative that you achieve this state of Alpha focus before iReading.

Autogenic Relaxation is an advanced method of mental relaxation. When properly utilized it will calm your mind by lowering its rate of functioning to a level between seven and twelve brain waves per second.

Just like the human fingerprint, every human mind is characterized by subtle differences in mental chemistry and structure and so, you may prefer one method of entering the alpha state over the other. The following can be used in the IMS or the IRS and vice versa, so adopt the technique that you feel suits you best and subplant it in your actions accordingly.

Autogenic Relaxation

1
As before, select a place where you can be alone and allow yourself to relax completely.

2
Close your eyes and breathe deeply, letting stress and anxiety flow out and harmony flow in with every breath. Allow your body to relax by releasing the tension flowing within your muscles and under the surface of your skin.

3

You must now begin to talk to the six parts of your body and guide each of them into relaxation: your left arm, your right arm, your left leg, your right leg, your chest and your head. The following language has been proven to work best.

Begin by repeating six times, one breath to one repetition (six breaths and six repetitions per body part), "My left arm is becoming heavy and warm." Then repeat six times, "My left arm is now heavy and warm." Finally, say six times, "My left arm is completely heavy and warm." Each time you inhale and exhale, you speak one command. Repeat this mantra for each of your other five body parts.

Breathe in: "My left arm is becoming heavy and warm."
Breathe out (repeat six times)
Breathe in: "My left arm is now heavy and warm."
Breathe out (repeat six times)
Breathe in: "My left arm is completely heavy and warm."
Breathe out (repeat six times)
Repeat this for the following five body parts: right arm, left leg, right leg, chest, head.

In less than 10 minutes, you will have talked your body into a deep state of relaxation. Feel the state overcome your physical body and flow from your head to your toe.

You should feel a certain heaviness and warmth to your body; this indicates that your blood vessels have relaxed and dilated. Such an experience of warmth influences your entire circulatory system, as the relaxation of your blood vessels will spread from your appendages to the coronary vessels. This results in a definite shifting of your body experience and induces results that are far superior to those of conventional relaxation techniques. At this point, your brain waves have slowed to a leisurely seven to twelve cycles per second—the Alpha state. You are now ready to focus on the given task. As with anything else, this advanced process of relaxation will become easier as you use it with an increasing capacity.

1.3
Act with Intention and Belief

The average individual never states his purpose or forms a conscious intention before reading. Articles, novels, texts and journals are seemingly picked up at random and then read—without any thought given to the why or the how. Such behavior can be likened to waking up in the morning and choosing to fill your day with arbitrarily determined tasks and events—like spending time getting dressed for the day and then choosing to have a shower. Behaving without a goal or intention is terribly inefficient.

Time is one of the most precious resources one has. Thus, anything less than a strategic plan on how you will spend it is plain uneconomical. Reading a book can take days, a long article more than an hour. Such time-consuming tasks should be managed as carefully as any other important job you do.

Before you start reading, silently state your purpose for reading the particular material. Francis Bacon once said, "Some books are to be tasted, others to be swallowed and some few to be chewed and digested." Many books demand to be read in their entirety, word by word, sentence by sen-

"Surviving and thriving as a professional today demands two new approaches to the written word. First, it requires a new approach to orchestrating information, by skillfully choosing what to read and what to ignore. Second, it requires a new approach to integrating information, by reading faster and with greater comprehension."
Jimmy Calano

tence. You might want to mull over each idea, savour each allegory and reflect on each composition. But there are also many books that one shouldn't read at all, plus all those that fall in between.

Those who choose to read Plato's *The Republic*, or Charles Dickens' *A Tale of Two Cities* would probably choose to read them in the traditional method of reading—one word at a time. But, if you are studying a 400-page text, you might want to tackle it through one rigorous exertion—by iReading.

"The man who does not read good books has no advantage over the man who cannot read them."
Mark Twain

Even if you wish to read Plato you might want to iRead it first to give you a subconscious preview of what the book entails. No matter what reading situation you are in, iReading can increase the quality of your experience. To act with intention, ask yourself the following questions before reading:

What am I expecting to achieve by reading this piece of work?

Are you looking to master a foreign language, learn a new software program, explore a current issue in greater depth, or enjoy the vivid prose of a classic novel? Establish exactly what it is you want to accomplish by reading the material.

How much of this material do I want to master? What level of detail do I want to get into?

Are you trying to memorize every distinguishable fact, remember the major themes of each chapter, or just the broad overtones of the reading? Establish this in advance of reading.

What are the benefits that can be had by reading this piece?

What are the expected outcomes associated with successfully reading this piece? If you intend to read a book to master a new language, what sort of benefits will you reap by doing so? Visualize what it will look like and emotionalize what it will feel like to achieve this goal.

What amount of time am I willing to spend on achieving this purpose?

What amount of time are you willing commit to achieve your reading goals? Are you willing to spend a month to pour over the *Guide to Learning Japanese*? Determine the length of time it will take to achieve your reading goal and then resolve to spend the necessary time, or not. In addition, make sure you keep within these time constraints.

As previously explained, creating intention in this manner will trigger an attractor within your mind to fulfill your intention. Your odds of accomplishing your mission will multiply as a result.

Mind Conditioning

Just as directed in the IMS, it is integral that you act in accordance with the Belief Maxim. "Whatever you believe with feeling and conviction becomes your reality." This maxim has jurisdiction over your whole existence and it must not be ignored.

Self-destructive thoughts must be dealt with and belief in the iReading system must be developed. Before continuing through the IRS process, **refer to Phase 1.2: Mind Conditioning.** Use the affirmations to the right, as well as

As I iRead, my concentration is a b s o l u t e and all that I read will be prgrammed into my mind for my future use.

I have the ability to master this proven technique and read at the speed of sight.

I have the ability to read a book in 20 minutes.

additional ones of your own creation, to strengthen your convictions and maximize your performance when iReading.

Progression Key

Now pick up your book and to prop it up at a 45-degree angle to the table or at a 90-degree angle to your eyes. As you prop it up, use a table or some sort of solid platform to rest your elbows in front, so your shoulders don't get sore. This will help you maintain a relaxed state throughout the duration of the reading.

1.4
Shift your Perspective

"Without shifting your perspective and changing the way you use your eyes, your infinite mind will not be tapped and your time will be wasted."

VTH

To visually capture the information on each page, you must undergo an alteration in your point of awareness and achieve a shift in perspective.

With the book in front of you, try imagining yourself floating just above and behind where you are currently sitting. You are suspended and hovering in full defiance of gravity; your eyes are looking at the book from a vantage point that is just above and slightly behind your head. Envision yourself gazing at the page from just behind yourself—as though you've psychologically stepped out of your physical body and your metaphysical self is leaning over the top of your physical self, peering at the page. This perspective will widen your field of sight, allowing you to capture fully both facing pages, the entire reading surface, with one glance.

As you gaze fixedly at the centre crease of the book, not only can you see the four corners of the book, but you can also see the things surrounding you by using your peripheral vision. Notice the room around you, not by shifting your eyes, but by maintaining a steady focus on the centre crease and using your peripheral vision. See the walls surrounding you, the floor beneath you and the ceiling above you. Try to keep your field of sight open and, again, notice the four corners of the book in your peripheral vision; see the full two pages, detect the four corners and gaze steadily at the centre crease. There should be a distinct clarity and focus to the book.

Now try to visualize an "X" connecting these four corners, with your gaze directed at the centre of this "X" While look-ing at the centre of this "X" soften your gaze and notice the white space surrounding the letters, the white space surround-ing the paragraphs and the pattern that the white space forms between the paragraphs. Maintain a strong awareness of the white space and the four corners while simply noticing the text. Maintain a soft gaze on these features of the book, never focusing intently on the text itself, all the while fixing your eyes on the centre of the "X".

The major intention of this step is to achieve divergent eyes. What are divergent eyes? When you normally read a book, your eyes converge on each word and sentence—hard focus-ing. When looking at your nose you are converging your eyes to the maximum extent as each eye points inward. When your eyes come together, they are converging.

Diverging your eyes means to split them apart, and so, to do so to the maximum extent would perhaps be to look at the moon or a far-off star. To achieve divergent eyes, you must make your eyes look forward in a broader capacity.

To achieve divergent eyes, with the book in your hands and in front of you, fix your gaze on a spot on the wall, beyond the top of the book. Your eyes are peering outward and your peripheral vision is allowing you to be fully aware of what is going on around you. Now slowly bring the book into your line of sight and as you do so, try to maintain your divergent focus on what is beyond the book. Imagine you have X-ray vision and can see clear through the centre crease. Beam your eyes right through the centre of the book at your focal plane beyond the centre crease as if you have laser sight. This will cause the plane of the book to look blurry and fuzzy. Keep this relaxed, divergent gaze and maintain this softer focus on the book.

Bring your attention to the blurriness that this divergent gaze creates around the centre crease and you will notice that there appears to be two centre creases, and between these two illusionary creases, a third page. Seeing this third page is a telltale sign that you have correctly shifted your perspective and have achieved divergent eyes.

At first, it will be difficult to maintain this third middle page. When you look beyond the book and slowly bring the book into your plane of sight, you may lose the third page quite easily. At first, move just the tip of the book into your line of sight to see the third page. You should be able to see it easily, but maintaining it takes some training. Practice keeping that third page in sight by moving the book slowly in and out of position, moving just the top of the book in and out of your line of sight. Practice closing your eyes for a few seconds and maintain the illusionary third page. Try blinking rapidly while keeping the third page in sight. By trying different things and putting in the necessary time, you will quickly become proficient at shifting your ocular focus. To train your eyes, refer to the section at the back of the book called "iReading Training."

Once you can see the illusionary third page that your eyes create and maintain its presence, you'll know that you have achieved the soft focus needed for iReading—and you'll have properly executed the first major step to unbounded information capture.

Progression Key

As a human being raised in our modern culture, you have surely been taught since birth to follow closely each word and sentence with strict concentration as you read. As children, many of us used our finger to follow along and many of us formed the habit of mouthing each word, or even reading aloud. It is our natural inclination to hard focus on each word and sentence. Going against this grain, as specified within this book, is going against a lifetime of customary convention and habit. Developing the ability to soft focus on a page and maintain such a focus for the remainder of a book takes practice. The temptation to focus in on words and sentences is strong at first, so you must train yourself to resist this tendency.

Realize this and resolve to gain the ability to attain a soft focus. You have the ability, it is just a matter of rewiring your eyes—by going against your natural instincts and practicing until it becomes second nature.

Using your eyes differently and maintaining your Alpha mind state as described allows the textual information to bypass your conscious mind and directly enter your subconscious. By keeping your eyes from forming a definite and hard focus and by directing your gaze at the centre of the page, you can engage your subconscious and capture the whole page of text.

1.5
iRead

Rhythmically Advance through the Material

You've achieved the necessary shift in perspective and it's now time to advance through the book. Beginning at the very beginning of the book (before the table of contents), start turning the page every two seconds in a steady tempo. This is the ideal pace for beginners.

As you turn, chant a specific phrase or mantra to keep yourself in rhythm:
1 . . . 2, turn; 1 . . . 2, turn; 1 . . . 2, turn;

Any phrase that can keep you to a steady pace is fine.
Re . . . lax, turn; Re . . . lax, turn;

Capture . . . the page, turn; Capture . . . the page, turn;

For the first several books you iRead, an entire 300-page book will take you 10 minutes, while a 600-page book will take 20 minutes. As you become more advanced, begin to turn the pages more quickly and spend as little as one second on each page. Advanced iReaders can work through a 600-page book in 10 minutes.

To maintain an achievement-oriented focus throughout the entire book, advance through the material with a steady mantra and in a rhythmic manner. With your breathing deep and even and your chant steady and rhythmic, you will maintain the Alpha state of mind, keep your subconscious engaged and capture the text fully.

As you progress through the book, keep your conscious mind free of negative thoughts and attention grabbers by gently deflecting them away and keeping your mind focused on your rhythmic chant.

Distractions and self-destructive thoughts can deter your focus and sabotage your performance. It is important to keep them at bay by catching them quickly and ridding them from your mind.

"Do not dwell in the past, do not dream of the future, concentrate the mind on the present moment."
Buddha

Continue to Gaze through the Words and Maintain Divergent Eyes

As you progress through the book, keep yourself from hard focusing on the text. Preserve your soft focus, sensing the four corners of the page and your fingers holding the book; see the illusionary third page, maintaining a strong awareness of the white space around the text; all the while, keep your eyes directed at the centre crease.

Close with Mastery

When you reach the very last page, close the book with a sense of mastery and belief. Be confident in the actions you've taken and know that by executing the process of iReading properly you will have fully swallowed the capsule of information the book represents; the information contained therein will be stored within your subconscious and will soon thereafter become part of your internal library of knowledge.

Take control of your thoughts and think in a positive manner. Repeat the mantra: "I release this information for my subconscious mind to process." Say it several times to begin the next part of the process effectively.

PROCESS TWO: ACTIVATE THE INFORMATION

By this point in the IRS procedure, you've learned how to effectively insert information directly and effectively into your subconscious. You've now entered process two of the Infinity Reading System; harness the power of EPI activation to breathe animation into your subconscious information database and transform the unprocessed information it contains into functional knowledge.

"When oil is drilled it's extracted from the earth in a raw and crude form. It isn't in a usable form until it goes through a refining process. The Infinity Reading System works in a similar manner."

VTH

2.6
Incubate

You've finished iReading the book, but before you activate the information, you must give the material time to incubate and simmer within the recesses of your mind. The information in the book is within your mind, but in its raw and unprocessed state, it is of no use, as it is scattered, disorganized and broken up. At a conscious level, it will appear that you know nothing of what you just iRead; all of the pieces to the puzzle are in your mind, but you need to put them together before you can create something of value.

Research has shown that you should wait a full 24 hours before beginning activation. A night of sleep allows your subconscious to consolidate quietly and format the new information. Although, if you are in circumstances that demand urgency, it is possible to activate 10 minutes after reading, although as a beginner you will not achieve the same results.

Research in Point

A breadth of research has led to the conclusion that learning skills consolidate in the brain during REM sleep. Your subconscious mind never rests and it will work through the material you've read extremely quickly—generating solutions and creating a vast network that intertwines the new information with your existing information databases, creating associations and linkages with your existing foundation of knowledge.

Performance of certain tasks actually improves the day after the new skill is learned, even when there has been no practice in between. A similar effect seems to occur with iReading.

"To read without reflecting is like eating without digesting."
Edmund Burke

2.7
Ignite Comprehension

After a period of incubation, you are ready to begin the second most important step in the iReading process: igniting comprehension. Trying to recall something after iReading is quite different than trying to recall something after conventional reading. Activation techniques are essential to stimulate recall; trying to force recall by searching your subconscious with your conscious mind will garner few results.

Just as iReading feeds the textual information into your

subconscious mind by a new method, it must be drawn out of your subconscious and into your conscious mind via a new method—you must create a conscious connection to the information in your subconscious by actively and purposefully pursuing that connection.

The text is used as a catalyst to stimulate the brain, so activation depends heavily on your levels of self-awareness; it is important to know what you're thinking, feeling and doing. At this juncture, you are familiar with the IMS and may have already made great progress in your developmental quest for an iMind. Your ability to communicate with the subconscious will have begun to blossom and will continue to do so, thereby making comprehension ignition increasingly easier.

As you go through the book as described below, you will be attracted to text relevant to the purpose for reading that you stated beforehand. Without having a purpose for reading a document, there is generally little that can come out of activation. Comprehension ignition creates a conscious directive to fulfill the goal you set earlier in the iReading process—whether it was mastery or simple understanding, activating the information will increase levels of comprehension. You may at first develop a heightened awareness and familiarity with the material, but once you are finished activation the desired level of knowledge will be achieved.

Positive Focus

With positive focus your vast subconscious mind will be free to use its natural ability to bring you the information you need and allow you to achieve the level of comprehension you desire. Self-Destructive Beliefs, or fear of failure, will only deter your effectiveness. Refer to the second step in the IRS process and act in accordance with the principles contained therein to attain a mental state of confident focus.

Ask Questions that Switch the Mind on

Before you begin EPI activation, start by asking yourself questions to get your subconscious working towards the best ways to activate the stored information. Stay relaxed, remain confident and feel the curiosity that these questions create within your mind.

What is important to me in that book I just read?

What do I need to know to perform well on the next test, to write my report, to lead the next meeting, or to be completely prepared for the next situation?

What valuable information might I find in what I just read?

The questions probe your mind for answers and stimulate action and curiosity within your subconscious, initiating the process of activating the information. Mind probing causes your subconscious to find the best means of creating comprehension on a conscious level, but it only begins the process of recall and comprehension. Don't expect an immediate and instantaneous answer to the questions you ask. To expect recall right away will only cause frustration.

EPI Activation

With the book open in front of you, you will explore the text like a detective, in a thoughtful and conscious manner. When you see a section of interest, focus your attention on it by probing for further clues. While probing, you may see a thought or idea that peaks your senses and grabs your interest. Do an intensive investigation by rapidly reading that area of text.

Progression Key

Open the text and, for the first time, turn to the table of contents commonly found at the beginning of the book. The table of contents is like a map of the book and with it you can anticipate a great deal of what you'll see during your exploration of the book. Become familiar with the map before you set out on your exploration of the text.

Explore

Explore the text, looking for the sections that grab your curiosity and interest; look for hints such as chapter titles, tables, subheadings or keywords.

Probe

Once you've found a section that you are curious about, begin to probe the pages of the text by quickly moving your eyes down the centre of the page, while trying to consciously recognize as many words as you can. The faster you go, the easier it is for your conscious mind to stay free from distraction.

Probing the page is done to accomplish one specific goal: to notice your attraction to words, thoughts and ideas on the page. This how your subconscious communicates what it finds meaningful and what is not.

The primary skill behind probing is to be sensitive to your mind's intuition as you scan the book. Follow your hunches, intuition and signals which tell you where to investigate. Your mind has been exposed to the entire book and all of the material contained therein, so allow your internal periphery of your awareness to be your guide. Allow yourself to be directed to the specific answers you search for. You may be attracted to a certain part of the page, as an inner voice tells you to stop and read.

As you probe the sections of interest, don't second-guess any urges you may have to dive in and investigate further. Signals arise for good reason and ignoring them would be a mistake. This is a universal law of your subconscious and doesn't apply only to this situation.

Investigate

Once probing has led you to a paragraph, sentence or page of the text that attracts you, begin to investigate the text in an in-depth manner. If you recall, the conscious mind only absorbs between five or nine (average is seven) chunks of information at once. Now is the time to read the text in an accelerated capacity, by maximizing your conscious forces. How do you read text at such an accelerated speed?

Accelerated Reading

Accelerated reading demands the ability to focus on a string of words (from five to nine) at a time—a skill that takes practice. The temptation to focus on single words is strong at first, so you must train yourself to resist this tendency.

To train your eyes, go to the beginning of this book. Starting at the first line of text, move your eyes across the page in an accelerated and smooth fashion. Advance your eyes over the words from left to right at an unswerving and steady rate, faster than you think you can handle. You want to break through hesitation and skepticism and burst through your comfort zone.

Try this for 15 minutes to train your eyes effectively and increase your scanning speed until you are spending roughly 10 seconds on each page. Doing this for only five minutes will not give you the same results.

As you scan through the reading at an accelerated pace, your internal system will be flooded with words and over-whelmed by the lines of seemingly blurry text. This stimulus can result in two different reactions.

1. You feel that you're not absorbing any of the reading and you feel that even if you continue to practice reading at this pace it will be impossible for you ever to do so. This will cause your mind to shut down and lessen its intensity. Your brain will be subverted by this belief and you will return to your habitual way of reading. No improvement will be made.

2. Your internal system becomes overwhelmed by the sheer amount of words you are visually soaking in. As you fight through this stage with positive expectations, your brain begins to adjust and to fine-tune its operation protocol. It begins to capture each word in a consistent flow, one after the other, rather than absorbing each word at a time. You begin to harness fully your conscious mind to soak up the reading

and ingest the text. This is the reflex that you must force to happen if you want to accelerate your reading.

Work to recognize the words and text, but don't verbally process them. See the words, but don't dwell on them. Capture the text at the maximum possible rate by *not* consciously zeroing in on each word. Recognize the words as symbols, just as you would if you saw a stop sign or an amber traffic light.

Resolve to gain the ability to attain a rapid focus on the text. Stop yourself from consciously engaging each independent word. Stretch your conscious abilities and allow this more efficient means of reading to feel more natural and authentic. Don't convert the text to sound and audio in your head—this causes you to read at the pace at which you talk, which is much slower.

With proper training you will find it more unnatural to interact with and consciously linger on every word, the way you habitually have. With a little practice, you will feel the words smoothly entering your mind without coaxing or reluctance.

You can set your mind to work like a quickly moving conveyor belt that continually feeds the information into your brain—bringing you to surge through the text with speed, consistency and efficiency, never faltering. You can configure your mind to work like this by overloading your senses until your senses adapt. Employ this universal law of adaptation to change your conscious processor of text.

It is important to continue with this exercise until you experience the second reaction to the stimulus; don't give up until you achieve this quantum leap in mental functioning.

You have the ability. It is just a matter of rewiring your eyes by going against your natural instincts and practicing until reading at an accelerated pace becomes second nature.

Capture the Thought, Not the Word

The secret to accelerated reading lies in the way you use your eyes to read whole phrases at a glance, not just single words. You want to see each chunk of written material as a full scene.

You want to learn to read longer groups of words (between five to nine) at a single glance, not just one, two or three words at a time. You will find that there is nothing difficult about this. All efficient readers do it.

For many, this is the most amazing discovery; with this alone, many individuals instantly double their base reading speed and, after some practice, going back to reading one or two words at a time became incredibly difficult.

Here is an illustration of the eye pauses made by slow, moderate and fast readers:

Slow: Some / poor / readers / actually / stop / look / and / think / after / nearly / every / word.

Moderate: Some poor readers / actually stop, look and think / after nearly every word.

Fast: Some poor readers actually stop, / look and think after nearly every word.

It is impossible to read quickly, with a great deal of comprehension, if you pause after every word. Each word is merely part of a whole thought and to understand written material well you must read for the thought, not for the individual words. The only way you can grasp thought units is by reading entire phrases (instead of words) at a single glance. Focus on what the writer is trying to say. Try to understand the point and the idea rather than letting each word register and radiate in your conscious mind as you read. Let the whole thought surface and intermingle with your own body of knowledge as you draw connections and associations.

Think how you move your eyes over a scenic landscape, such as Niagara Falls. You move your eyes smoothly and fluidly from one side to the other, seeing all the colors, sizes, shapes, movement and splendour. You don't stop to examine or focus on a part of the scenery, but you move your eyes smoothly across the landscape. You move your eyes across the page in much the same manner, as you smoothly absorb each three-to-seven-word chunk by scanning your eyes over each unit of thought. Don't hard focus on one word more than another; rather, effortlessly and smoothly move your eyes across the page.

As before, go to the beginning of this section and practice absorbing groups of words at a time—start by capturing two words at once. Once you master this, you can gradually progress to reading entire phrases at once.

As presented earlier, research shows the conscious mind can process five to nine chunks of information at a time and, thus, capturing on average seven words at a time is the recommended pace for optimal accelerated reading while maintaining excellent comprehension.

Progression Key

You must familiarize yourself with reading complete thoughts at a glance. It is important to practice this activity on a continual basis, even if you aren't iReading the material beforehand.

Remember, when you try to read faster you are trying to get rid of all unnecessary pauses. Any pause is unnecessary. Phrase-reading will not only dramatically increase your reading speed but will also force you to concentrate more. An increase in concentration combined with the effect of reading for thoughts will immensely improve your comprehension.

Look for Changes in Thought

As you capture each phrase and read for thought, you must look for signposts. Signposts indicate a change in thought and argument. They are words such as: *but, despite, on the contrary, however, nonetheless, yet and rather.* As you see these words you will know that the author is about to introduce a contradictory thought, which will cause you to take special notice of this change in argument.

You must also look for go-ahead signals. They indicate that a similar thought will be expressed. Go-ahead signals are words such as: *and, moreover, furthermore, also, likewise, thus, therefore, consequently and accordingly.* Go-ahead signals cause you to quickly skip over the next section, as you will usually find redundant information.

Accelerated Reading Overview

At first you may feel that your reading comprehension dips. Rest assured that with practice your mind will soon catch on and as your skill grows, your comprehension will become even better than it has ever been.

In addition, it may seem that the words are out of focus and fuzzy when moving your eyes at an accelerated rate. Don't try to clear this up. Just continue to move your eyes smoothly and steadily over the print with a natural flow. The print will clear up with practice.

Remember: you won't focus your eyes on every single word when reading at an optimum speed and, thus, it may feel like you are missing certain words altogether. Due to your previously ingrained habit of reading one or two words at a time, you may feel that you are missing valuable information and begin to pull yourself back to a slower pace. Don't give in to this temptation and never let this happen. You can assure yourself that your comprehension is not suffering—rather, you are simply at the base of a steeply rising learning curve. While you are learning the skill of Accelerated Reading, your previous habits are still guiding your thoughts and actions. You still believe that you must consciously see every word in order to understand the sentence. This isn't true.

The reality of this is easily identifiable in the context of conversation. Do you need to hear every word your friend says to grasp the intention of what he is communicating? Many times, all one needs to hear is one of several words to capture the meaning of what is being said. Everyone has experienced this. Perhaps your father is mowing the lawn and he calls you over but all you can make out from his muffled shouts is "water." By observing the context and body language of your father, you naturally infer that he wants a cold glass of water.

At the opposite end of the spectrum are those situations in which you unnecessarily ask a person to repeat herself/himself. How many times has someone asked you a question and your automatic response was, "Pardon?" even though you understood what was being said? Perhaps you didn't clearly hear one of several words spoken and, before you even realize it, you ask that person to repeat the statement. Usually, you quickly realize that you did understand what was said and sometimes feel a little silly for asking for clarification.

While in discussion, extremely intelligent people can often anticipate the point someone is about to make, or the statement that is about to be communicated. The fact is that your mind works faster than the pace at which you hear and talk. These constants apply to reading as well.

Progression Key

Once your curiosity in a certain area has been quenched, continue to probe through that section in the book or begin to explore the book looking for a new section of interest. Don't make an effort to memorize the content—this interferes. Remember, you already have all the information in your mind and activation is intended to bring it all together for you.

Ignite Comprehension Overview

Switching your mind on through questioning should have made you curious about certain topics, sections or passages in the text. Perhaps you've iRead a book on international business ethics and your primary goal was to develop a greater understanding on East Asian business practices. You would have asked some questions about this topic when scanning your mind—and you would want to go to the section of the book that deals with this topic.

Reading experts estimate that 90 percent of any text is filler—thereby making roughly 9/10ths of anything you read only interesting commentary. EPI activation will lead you directly to the substantive 1/10th of the material and, for this reason, don't give into the urge to probe and investigate everything. When skipping pages don't give in to the feeling that you are missing something; it is natural to feel this, but fight the urge and don't give in to your old habits of reading.

Explore the book and turn to the sections that grab your curiosity and interest. Look for hints, such as chapter titles, tables, subheadings, or keywords to find the sections that contain the content which pertains directly to the knowledge you most want to get out of the text.

In these sections, rapidly scan your eyes down the center of each page and probe the material. If any word or phrase catches your eye, investigate the page and read in an accelerated speed until you are satisfied. Then resume your probing pattern by quickly moving your eyes over the centre of the page.

Igniting comprehension can be achieved by many different ways; EPI activation is only one of them. Another way to ignite comprehension is to call upon the IMS to visualize your iReading experience. Envision yourself opening the cover of the book, then describe what you sense, feel, see and experience there. This will cause your subconscious to call into action the crude information stored in its database, sift through it and thereby begin the creation of comprehension.

You want to ration each investigation to a paragraph or two in a short piece of writing, or a page or two in any large text. Follow your hunches, not your logic. Allow your subconscious to direct your investigations into the text, even if the passage seems irrelevant to your purpose. If you mistrust your initial hunches or want greater thoroughness, probe and investigate the entire text from the first to the last page. Each time you probe and investigate, you are becoming more familiar with the text, as you trigger greater comprehension.

Progression Key

With a few guided runs through the Infinity Reading System, the process will be experientially ingrained in your mind so that continual reference will be unnecessary.

"Practice doesn't make perfect. Perfect practice makes perfect."
Vince Lombardi

As your mind ascends higher up the learning curve, your self-limiting beliefs about your reading ability will be cast away and replaced by thoughts of self-liberation. Once you reach this level, it is only a matter of time until you master the system of iReading. The quicker you are able to achieve this level, the larger your internal library of knowledge will become.

IMAGINE HAVING A PORSCHE 911 IN YOUR GARAGE. A CAR SO FANTASTIC, IT HAS ALMOST A SUPERNATURAL HOLD ON YOUR THOUGHTS; YOU WANT SO BADLY TO TURN THE IGNITION, CRANK THE ACCELERATOR, ZOOM AWAY FOR THE DAY, AND ENJOY THIS ULTIMATE DRIVING MACHINE, BUT YOU CAN'T. YOU SEE, THE PORSCHE HAS A MASSIVE 12-CYLINDER ENGINE UNDER THE HOOD, BUT YOU DON'T HAVE THE KEY. YOU PEER THROUGH THE GLASS, ADMIRE THE STYLED INTERIOR, AND MARVEL OVER THE CONTOURED BODY, BUT YOU HAVE NO WAY OF STARTING THIS BEAUTIFUL CAR AND IGNITING THE POWERFUL ENGINE UNDER-NEATH THE HOOD. IF ONLY IT WERE ACCES-SIBLE, YOU KNOW YOU WOULD HAVE THE TIME OF YOUR LIFE, BUT WITHOUT THE KEY, IT SITS—UNUSED AND UNTAPPED.

THE INFINITY READING SYSTEM IS THE KEY TO YOUR INTERNAL SUBCONSCIOUS ENGINE; AND NOT UNLIKE THE SHEER FORCE OF A PORSCHE 911, IF THIS KEY IS USED, YOU WILL BEGIN TO PROCESS INFORMATION AT AN UNEQUALLED LEVEL, FAST TRACKING YOUR LIFE TO UNBOUNDED ACHIEVEMENT.

phase shift

Phase Four

The knowledge you now command must still be put into action. Don't seek out information only to remain stagnant, only to continue existing in your accustomed mode of operation. Those who fail to act effectively on new information and knowledge stunt all growth and development; they can never improve because they factor knowledge out of the equation.

ACTION IS THE DISTINGUISHING FACTOR BETWEEN THOSE WHO RISE UP TO CLAIM THAT OF WHICH THEY ARE CAPABLE AND THOSE WHO DON'T.

You must put the stratagem you've learned into action. You must call upon the wisdom you control. You've learned to accelerate your mind. You've acquired strategy to operate in a heightened capacity.

MAKE A COMMITMENT TO PUT INTO ACTION WHAT YOU'VE LEARNED AND INITIATE A NEW LEVEL OF EXISTENCE. LET WISDOM GUIDE YOUR ACTIONS AND IMPROVE YOUR EFFECTIVENESS. LET IT REVOLUTIONIZE YOUR THOUGHT PROCESSES, BROADEN YOUR OUTLOOK, AND POWER YOU TO SUCCESS.

This is the integral step in personal evolution. Anyone can read a book or hear a wise man speak—but not anyone can insert that wisdom into their internal realm, change their human system and transfer that into a real, measurable improvement in effectiveness. Guide your mind to a mode conducive to forward movement and activate your internal trigger for action.

PHASE 4 WILL HELP YOU CHOOSE THE GOALS AND MISSIONS OF YOUR FUTURE AND CHARGE YOUR INTERNAL SYSTEM WITH THESE OBJECTIVES, CONDITIONING YOU FOR SKILLFUL AND DRIVEN ACTION.

PROGRESSION SCHEDULE

Day ten **Action**

    4.1 Goal Creation

Day eleven **Action**

    4.1 Goal Configuration Atlas

Day twelve **Action**

    4.1 Goal Charging

Goal Conditioning

Goals: constant directors of thought and action

Human beings are success-driven, ambition-fuelled organisms. The human machine is by design a goal-seeking mechanism. We can exist without possessing a purpose in life, but never live. Without goals we will wander aimlessly and self-destruct. Humans need targets and objectives to flourish—goals provide these, as they direct our actions and awaken our energy levels.

"You must infuse purpose into your mind to act purposefully."
VTH

Goals charge us with desire and work to push us outside our comfort zones, causing us to challenge ourselves and expand. They give us the momentum to advance even when things are distressing or seemingly insurmountable. The individual with strong goals and a clear image of desire causes these elements, through repetition, to become deeply embedded within his or her subconscious mind and is therefore enabled, due to the mind's generative and sustaining power, to attain his/her goals in the least amount of time and with the least amount of physical exertion. They accelerate our subconscious activity, harnessing its powers of achievement, causing us to unconsciously zero in on our target 24 hours a day, 365 days a year. Just focus your thought forces unceasingly. Little by little you will achieve actualization, as all your abilities and mental powers become engaged to that end.

"Make your life a mission —not an intermission."
Arnold Glasgow

In North America today, only five percent of the population has formed goals for their future, and only one percent have actually taken the effort to write them down. Approximately 99 percent of the people in our society do not have clear, concise, written goals. The average person spends more time planning their vacation, a party, studying the newspaper, or making a Christmas list than they do planning their lives.

"It concerns us to know the purposes we seek in life, for then, like archers aiming at a definite mark, we shall be more likely to attain what we want."

Aristotle

Fulfillment or success has been defined as the progressive realization of goals that are worthy of the individual. By failing to forge a decisive action plan you will never succeed. Living without goals is like traveling towards your destination, your imagined and dreamed "Acropolis of Success" without fuel in your tank. You know you would like to get there, but you never will.

Think of a Major League, Cy Young Award-winning pitcher—so gifted at his craft that he can throw a split-fingered curve ball right down the pipe, nailing the catcher's glove, and then, take a second ball and blow a 105-mph fastball by an all-star hitter. Now picture that same exceptional pitcher, at the top of his sport, but blind-folded and then spun around several times before taking aim for that catcher. How well would that extremely talented athlete perform? Now you may be asking yourself, how could he take aim and hit a target that he can't even see. The real question is: How can anyone hit a target they can't see? How can YOU hit a target you don't even have? Do you have your targets?

Case in Point

A study conducted in 1953 on the senior graduating class of Yale University highlights the power of goal setting. The graduates were given a survey that asked, among other questions, "Have you written down, on paper, your specific goals, with detailed plans of action for achieving those goals?" The researchers found that only three percent of the graduating class had done these things.

They followed the graduates of the class of '55 and in 1973 they followed up the study; the results they found were startling. By measure of financial wealth and career accomplishments, they found that, of the total graduating class, the three percent who answered yes to having specific goals and detailed action plans had compiled more wealth, a greater net worth and more career success than the other 97 percent. What is also interesting was that these three percent were reported to have been more personally fulfilled, led happier lives, and lived longer than the rest of their peers. This truly epitomizes the influence goal setting can have on your future—an individual's worth is no greater than his or her ambitions.

"Give me a stock clerk with a goal and I will give you someone who will make history —give me someone without a goal and I will give you a stock clerk.."

J.C. Penney

Progression Key

Techniques that tap your internal source of drive and passion, accelerate human action and maximize individual goal attainment have been put to use by leading minds since the dawn of thought.

The advent of the Information Age has uncovered these strategies, and their recent fusion with cutting-edge psychological research has created the system of "Goal

Conditioning"—introduced here for your personal use. The three-part system of Goal Conditioning is an interactive guide to designing and achieving goals in your life.

"When there is no vision the people perish."
Proverbs 29:18

It is essential to execute each following exercise with an intense desire for improvement, absolute trust in the process and patient persistence. You must make a commitment to Goal Conditioning, forcing yourself to follow through to utilize fully the potential for accomplishment this system offers.

Goal Creation

Without goals and plans to reach them, you are like a ship without a rudder, sometimes drifting aimlessly and sometimes going full steam ahead in random directions. Those without purpose accomplish very little over a lifetime. They tend to be very busy, always moving, going, spending, doing. They confuse busyness with accomplishment—busy people, with no goals or direction, only accomplish busyness.

"The cynic knows the price of every-thing and the value of nothing."
Oscar Wilde

Goals can only be achieved once they're conceived. If you haven't created your goals, then you're taking action in random areas of existence and completing random tasks—not accomplishing and advancing. The Mind Accelerator is designed to bolster your actions and power-assist in your quest for excellence—if you haven't begun your quest, begin it now. The following will guide you through goal creation.

Step 1
Ask yourself, "What are the five things I value most in life?" The answer will shed light on that which you cherish and treasure; this is valuable information when forging specialized goals.

Step 2

In 30 seconds or less, write down your three biggest dreams of the moment—those about which you fantasize during lazy summer afternoons and those about which you daydream during boring mornings at school or work. Or conversely, imagine that you received one wish from a genie. What one great thing would you wish for, if you knew you could not fail?

Try to think of a few different wishes and dreams that you would pursue if given this wondrous opportunity and write them down. Each of these wishes can be interpreted as a goal worth accomplishing—a goal that is very much associated with who you would like to become in the future. By evaluating your answers to this question, you will have gained a greater window of insight into what it is you want to accomplish.

_____

_____

_____

_____

_____

_____

_____

_____

_____

_____

"Develop a burning desire to learn: The foundation of successful learning lies in motivation. Once you've built this foundation—a strong desire to learn—you will begin to feed this passion and build the walls of the house—the basic mental structure of an educated individual. You will never cease to grow, always becoming a more complete and enlightened person."

VTH

Step 3

What would you do if you won the lottery tomorrow? What would you change in your life? Visualize it and write down a quick description.

What would you do if you had no limitations at all and you could become anyone or do anything? Again, write it down.

_____

_____

_____

_____

_____

_____

_____

_____

_____

_____

The very fact that you can write answers to these questions and visualize extraordinary things occurring in your life, means you can accomplish these things.

Step 4

What would you do if you learned that you only had six months to live? Where would you want to go, what would you want to see, who would you want to spend time with, what things would you want to accomplish and how would you want to be remembered?

Write down as many things as you can think of, as these things may help indicate what is most important to you. That which you write down should be incorporated into your usual life activities.

_____

_____

_____

_____

Step 5

What have you always wanted to do but have been too afraid
to try? If you could eliminate all internal fears, what one
activity would you set out to conquer first?

_____

_____

_____

_____

_____

_____

_____

_____

_____

Step 6

In looking back at all the things that you have done in your
life, what has given you the most rewarding experience, the
most satisfaction, the greatest feeling of self-worth and
importance? Did you ever engage in an activity, environment,
situation, action, adventure, journey, sport, undertaking, project, or investment that made you feel great inside?

*"A person
who aims at
nothing is
sure to hit it."*
Anon.

_____

_____

_____

_____

_____

_____

_____

_____

_____

Step 7

At this time, you should have a good idea of some long-term goals you want to accomplish. Write these preliminary goals down here.

_____

_____

_____

_____

"We will
either find a
way, or make
one."

_____

_____

Hannibal

_____

_____

_____

_____

Step 8

Look above: for each goal you've written down, determine the price, both internal and external, that you will have to pay to realize it. Investigate the toll that each goal will take. Explore the pain you may feel while working toward each goal. Dream of the glories each goal will bring, and think of the pleasure that will come from progressing towards your goal and finally achieving it.

Delve into both sides of the divide and understand the double-edged sword that each goal represents.

Step 9

You've formulated some goals, now ask yourself these questions:

Is it really the goal I want to achieve?

Are my short-range goals consistent with my long-range goals? Can I commit myself emotionally to achieving these outcomes? Do I really have the intense desire needed to accomplish them? Can I visualize myself reaching this goal? Is my goal an end in itself, or simply a means to an end? For example, is your long-term goal of landing a top job in sales just that, or is it simply a way to afford the luxury and material needs you desire? If it is, identify the long-term, end goal and then outline each goal you must accomplish to end up there. "Business Degree + Sales Employment + High Sales Performance = the *Beneteau Oceanis* Yacht and the Ferrari 360 Spider exotic sports car you ultimately want as your long-term goal."

Is my goal elusive or substantive? The former is: "lose weight." The latter is: "walk 30 minutes three times a week," or "stop eating ice cream after dinner." That's a real plan of action. Powerful results come from specific actions that have measurable results.

Revisit your list of goals and shorten that list. Say "no" to the fine and yes to the finest. Research has shown that you can work on up to 15 goals at once, so if you have more than this, cut them down at this time.

Step 10
Develop desire
For each goal you've conceived, visualize all the pleasure that comes with working towards and achieving it. Emotionalize the feeling of victory and deliverance you will experience on that final day of reckoning.

Ignite an intense burning desire and enthusiasm for your goal by taking part in these emotions. Any triumph the world has ever witnessed was an act of desire and enthusiasm. Enthusiasm gives any act, challenge, or occupation meaning and significance—in its absence, anything that demands effort and dedication is unachievable. Desire injects spirit and heart into your movements—without it, your efforts will be muted and the accomplishment numbed.

Step 11
Determine how you will benefit from achieving your goal
Make a list of every benefit you will receive directly from achieving your goal. Think in terms of personal growth, financial condition, academia and every other area of your life.

Can you think of any reasons why you won't benefit from your goal? Maybe your goal is to become a doctor; a possible concern is the debt you could incur doing so and the long hours of work it requires.

Once you have finished this process, ask yourself if there are enough reasons for you to commit to this goal. Decide whether or not it's worth doing. Make a firm decision one way or the other.

Step 12
Develop absolute belief of attainability
You will only achieve it, if you believe in it. Never tell yourself, "It'll never happen." We have all seen our lives change in a heartbeat—sometimes an upturn and sometimes a downturn. But generally, success towards any goal is a longer road that takes daily work to make it a reality. It will happen.

Don't expect it to happen overnight, but expect it to happen.

Make the decision in advance that you will never, ever give up. Powerful results come from taking baby steps, one after another, day after day, until you reach your goal. That huge biology final exam may seem insurmountable, but by working through it in small increments, anything can become manageable. Never cast a shadow of self-doubt, otherwise you have already failed. Like a heat-seeking missile, you've determined your target, and nothing can stop you from striking it, unless you let it.

"I've never met anyone who isn't capable of achieving the most daring goals—but I've met many who never will because they've never set them."
Taylor Andrew Wilson

Step 13
Record your future course
At this point, you should have a strong vision of what you want your future to hold: an excellent idea of the targets and goals you want to accomplish. Take a few moments to transcribe carefully the goals you've created into the space provided. They will be used in the next exercise.

_____

_____

_____

_____

_____

_____

_____

_____

Let that inkling feeling of happiness come over you and welcome it. With a concrete list of goals, you've now bridged the gap between the dreamers and the achievers, and suddenly success is no longer a universe away, but right in front of you.

Key to Use

Use Goal Creation to create goals worthy of your efforts. With strategy to expand your IQ and absorb information at an astounding pace, now is an excellent time to re-evaluate your direction in life. You might have been underestimating your abilities up to this point and therefore set goals of lesser ambition, or you might not have set goals at all.

Stop undershooting and create goals that will accelerate your mind and drive you to higher levels of functioning. Set goals to improve your abilities and aptitudes using the strategies you are now familiar with. With a higher capacity to perform, you will gain the ability to take action with incredible effectiveness and achieve virtually any goal you set. Remember, every peak-performing individual is an avid, systematic and habitual goal setter. By forming and truly believing in your goals, you will self-activate your force for success.

"Ideas must work through the brains and the arms of good, brave men, or they are no better than dreams."
Ralph Waldo Emerson

Goal Configuration Atlas
10 Steps to develop your GCA

A recent study found that 65 percent of all college students in the United States think they will become millionaires. Most of these students feel that they deserve it already, having done not a thing towards that goal other than showing up for class—with one eye shut and maybe even both. The truth is that less than three percent of them will ever reach that mark. But when the remaining 97 percent of those students reach 40 and haven't reached the millionaire mark, the majority will feel like absolute failures. But what these students didn't know was that they never even had a chance of meeting that target; they simply didn't take the necessary steps to map out their future and achieve their goals.

The Goal Configuration Atlas is your tool for crafting the most complete and effective map for goal attainment. Before the archer can strike the bull's-eye, he must first construct his bow, fashion his quiver, load his arrow, aim his bow, retract his arm and release—only then can he strike his target. You must do the same. The GCA is your detailed action plan of advancement, plotting out your short-term and long-term future course. This graphical instrument is shaped like a pyramid, designed for you to first fill in your long-term goal at the peak of the pyramid and then create the underlying structure that supports the accomplishment of that goal. Just as you would do when building a pyramid, you must create a base strong enough to support the critical height you expect the apex to reach.

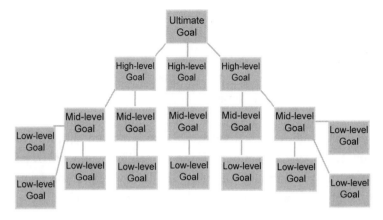

This flow chart should give you insight into the architectural construction of a GCA. Your GCA can have any number of layers and each layer of the GCA can contain as many goals as you need it to. You can build up your GCA to an enormous extent, planning the next few weeks, five years, or 20 years of your life and filling a whole wall if you feel so compelled. Build such a structure for yourself by going through the steps shown below.

Step 1

Begin constructing your GCA by determining your long-term, ultimate goals. These end goals will be placed at the apex of the GCA—at the top of the pyramid. These are goals that are supported by all those that will go underneath. Place any number of goals at the top, but ensure that they really belong at the top. If a goal can be seen as a supporting action for a desired effect, then that effect should be identified and inserted into your GCA. At this point, add the support for your top goal by forming a layer of high-end goals beneath.

Step 2

Begin to fill in the underpinning, supporting framework for

your high-level goals—the necessary goals that are directly supportive of the high-level goals—goals that need to be achieved directly before your end goal can be accomplished. These goals that go directly underneath your high-level goals will be your mid-level goals.

These mid-level goals may be somewhat ambiguous and uncertain in some cases. This is expected, but you want to do the best you can in filling them in. If you need to do some research to gain a greater understanding of what the high-level goals demand, it is best to do so at this point.

Step 3

Once you finish filling in your mid-level goals, begin to fill in your low-level goals. These low-level goals will be as short term as possible. You should have a precise understanding of the short-term action your mid- and high-level goals necessitate, and this should be reflected in your GCA.

The low-level goals should generally consist of accomplishments that can be achieved within the next month to 12 months. The more detail in your GCA, the better your action plan. Detail is a quality that all successful individuals pay mind to when thinking about their future.

Step 4

Analyze your starting point

Evaluate your current position, where you stand now. How far along are you? What makes your current situation favourable? Where you are currently situated may contain inherent opportunities that give you leverage in achieving your goals.

"View every goal as an action that supports future achievement. A low-level goal such as "Eat tuna and egg whites for breakfast each morning" is really an action that supports a higher-level goal such as "To finish a 20-km marathon." And this goal is really an action that supports a goal such as "Maintain nine percent body fat," which in turn is an action that supports a goal such as "Attend my great-grand-child's wedding."

VTH

Step 5
Set a deadline
For every goal, attach a deadline by which you will have accomplished your goals. Ensure it is reasonable, but not drawn out and extended. This will be the yardstick by which you can measure your progress.

"Do what you can, with what you have, where you are."
Theodore Roosevelt

You can be flexible with your deadlines. For a high-level goal, it may be a two- or even five-year gap, while low-level goals may carry a deadline as definite as a certain day.

Step 6
Identify the obstacles that stand in your way
Make a list of barriers, potential roadblocks and constraints between you and the accomplishment of your goal. For example, do you have the resources needed to accomplish your goal (money, time, etc.)? Once you've identified these barriers, determine how each obstacle can be overcome (loan from bank, quit your part-time job, etc.). Knowing the challenge that lies ahead will increase your odds of overcoming it.

Step 7
Identify the additional information and knowledge you will require to achieve your goal. To which books, courses or sources of information must you gain access? Are there any specific people from whom you could seek information?

Step 8
Identify all the people whose help and co-operation you will require. Whom must you contact and get on your side to achieve your goal? It might be the bank for a student loan or your parents for tuition.

Key to use

Creating a GCA for your future not only plots out your future course, but it creates a clear, linear and sequential campaign of action. The interrelatedness and associative connections the GCA fabricates also embed greater desire in your mind, as you unconsciously attach immediate action to high-level goal accomplishment.

This has been proven to be the most effective method to create an action plan for goal capture and format your sub-conscious for immediate action—your subconscious can clearly organize your future path and unconsciously navigate your progression towards your end goals.

As you work your way through the goals contained therein, strike them off as they're achieved, while adding to the detail and accuracy of goals as you approach them. As you progress, you might want to rewrite your GCA to adjust for changes and add detail. Feel free to do so.

Refer to your GCA often, for it is your future that can be found there. Synchronize your efforts and action with the flow of events that the GCA represents, and you will quickly move towards your high-level goals and live at the very top of the pyramid. Post it above your work space on a bulletin board, or like a poster on the wall; this will reinforce the high priority of your action plan.

Successful individuals know the goals they desire to achieve and construct plans of action to do so. They know that suc-cessful achievement of their goals will occur only when "opportunity meets preparation"—and opportunity will only show itself to those who are equipped to take advantage of it. This is one of those opportunities. Will you take advantage of it, or will you pass it over like so many other average-achieving individuals?

Research in Point

"Dost thou love life, then do not squander time, for that's the stuff life is made of."

Benjamin Franklin

Physically recording your goals is a powerful way to imprint them on your subconscious mind; even done once, for example as a New Year's resolution, it will produce fitting results. Those who took part in a test group found, when rereading the list at the end of the year, they had accomplished some of their New Year's goals. Imagine how many you could accomplish if you reviewed and continued to affirm these goals several times a week. By boosting your force for success, by way of planting beautiful, tiny little seeds, your mind will blossom into a garden of genius—and life will become your bountiful harvest.

Goal Charging

KEY SUCCESS STRATEGY
engage every 24 hours

"Nothing great will ever be achieved without great men and men are great only if they are determined to be so."

Charles De Gaulle

By harnessing your mind's power of simulation, you can imagine total achievement and mentally rehearse complete success. Your subconscious will merely accept the mental picture as a command to guide future action. German athletes used this in their preparation for the Olympic Games—they visualized their winning moments. This method is now used by virtually every successful Olympic athlete and by most gold-medal-winning competitors.

At this point, you have created and configured goals worthy

of your time, energy and ambitions—you are now ready to program these ambitions into your subconscious. The following system of "Goal Charging" will program goals into your mind, feeding it with the aspiration and desire for which it hungers. Just as a battery gains its strength when you charge it with energy, your mind becomes bolstered by the positive mental energy that goals provide.

Step 1

Just as you've done in the previous exercise, the process begins by calibrating your rate of thought and dropping down into a more meditative state of mind.

In the most quiet and peaceful place possible, sit comfortably and take several deep inhalations, followed by several deep and slow exhalations; at the same time, rhythmically repeat the word "relax." Do this over a 30-second period to relax your body and prepare your mind for conditioning.

After spending approximately 30 seconds doing this, your brain will quickly fall into its Alpha state. To achieve this narrow and relaxed mental focus takes some practice and discipline, but it is completely essential, as it causes your subconscious mind to be opened up and prepared to absorb the coming messages.

Step 2

Get out your completed Goal Configuration Atlas. Beginning with the first of your low-level goals, begin to verbalize and assert the desired outcome. Repeat a statement that clearly and simply describes your low-level goal. If a low-level goal happens to be "Achieve an 'A' grade on business exam," then

"All growth depends upon activity. There is no development physically or intellectually without effort and effort means work. Work is not a curse; it is the prerogative of intelligence, the only means to manhood and the measure of civilization."
Calvin Coolidge

"Obstacles are those frightful things you see when you take your eyes off your goal."
Henry Ford

you would verbalize, "I will achieve an 'A' grade on my business exam." Verbalize the goal five times. Tell yourself that you will grapple courageously with the goal you are preparing for and come out on top.

Step 3
Visualize yourself achieving that goal, accomplishing the task and succeeding victoriously.

What will be your final action? How will you look when you achieve the ultimate goal? Who will be with you? What will you do? Clearly see the outcome you desire, including yourself and everyone else who may be involved.

Step 4
Smile and emotionalize the pleasure that will accompany the achievement of your goal. Create the feelings of pleasure and happiness that will ensue once your goal is attained. Simulate the feeling you will experience when the desired outcome is reached. Imagine yourself already successful and the goal already attained. Commit, and resolve to pay the price in order to achieve the goal.

Step 5
Refer back to Step 2 and repeat this entire process for your remaining low-level goals, then begin to do the same for your mid-level goals. Finally, go through the entire process for your high-level goals, causing you to charge effectively the whole GCA into your mind.

Step 6
When you have completed the previous steps for each of your low-, mid- and high-level goals, visualize yourself successfully

navigating the GCA and achieving each goal in succession. Imagine yourself decisively striking off each goal as you slowly climb the pyramid to ultimate success. What will be your final action? How will you look when you achieve the ultimate high-level goal? Who will be with you, what will you do? Commit, and resolve to pay the price in order to achieve these goals.

Step 7

Just as you did before, release all concern, exhale and confidently release the goal from your mind—this is the catalyst in the process. Let it go, just as you would if someone you trusted said to you that you would be successful at achieving your goal and that you shouldn't worry about it again. You will feel an overwhelming sense of purpose. Bask in it and let it drive your actions.

Repeat the process for each goal in your GCA. Your subconscious can work effectively on 10 to 15 goals at once. It should take only 30 to 60 seconds for each goal and no more than 15 minutes for 15 goals. Use Goal Charging once a day, preferably every morning, to program your subconscious for action.

Key to use

Repeat the process for each goal in your GCA. Remember, your subconscious can work effectively on 10 to 15 goals at once. It should take only 30-60 seconds for each goal, and no more than 15 minutes for 15 goals. Use Goal Charging once a day, a preferably every morning to program your subconscious for action.

YOU'VE NOW COMPLETED THE GOAL CONDITIONING SYSTEM—THE PROGRESS YOU'VE MADE HAS BEGUN TO REVOLUTIONIZE YOUR THOUGHT PATTERNS AND RETOOL YOUR INTERNAL GUIDANCE SYSTEM.

CONTINUALLY USING THIS SYSTEM WILL FURTHER STRENGTHEN YOUR VOLITION FOR SUCCESS.

YOU ARE ONLY WEEKS, POTENTIALLY DAYS, FROM YOUR FIRST INITIATION OF SUCCESS.

BY MAINTAINING THE HABITS OF A SYSTEMATIC GOAL SETTER AND FREQUENTLY USING THE GOAL CONDITIONING STRATEGY, YOU WILL BEGIN TO CAPTURE ACHIEVEMENT, GARNER GREAT SUCCESS, AND SOLIDIFY YOURSELF ON THE PERPETUAL PATH OF SUCCESS.

AS THOMAS JEFFERSON ONCE SAID, "NOTHING CAN STOP THE MAN WITH THE RIGHT MENTAL ATTITUDE FROM ACHIEVING HIS GOAL."

IT'S BEEN 12 DAYS SINCE FIRST ENGAGING PHASE ONE. SINCE THEN, YOU'VE STARTED A REVOLUTION IN YOUR IDENTITY, CREATING A DIMENSIONAL RIFT BETWEEN THE PERSON YOU WERE 12 DAYS AGO AND THE PERSON YOU ARE NOW. WITH YOUR FORCE FOR SUCCESS GAINING STRENGTH BY THE HOUR, AND A NATURAL GENIUS THAT YOU'VE ONLY BEGUN TO DISCOVER, YOU ARE READY TO VENTURE OUT AND BEGIN YOUR NEW EXISTENCE. WITH YOUR NEW SET OF EYES, YOU'RE READY TO ACT AND ENGAGE THE WORLD WITH RENEWED PURPOSE.

your journey begins

This guided journey is now over, but your own has just begun. This manual of mind acceleration is but a beginning—learning is only the first leg of your quest. What you've learned must still be put into action. Don't absorb information only to remain stagnant, only to continue existing in your accustomed mode of operation. Those who fail to act on new information and knowledge effectively stunt all growth and development. They can never improve because they factor knowledge out of the equation.

You must put what you've learned into action. You must call upon the wisdom you control. You've learned to accelerate your mind and you've acquired the strategy to operate in a heightened capacity. Make a commitment to put into action what you've learned and initiate a new level of existence; let wisdom guide your action, revolutionize your thought processes, broaden your outlook, and empower you for success.

It takes a certain dedication to excellence to insert this strategy into your internal realm, change your internal system, and transfer that volition into real, measurable improvement in your results. Hindsight is always 20/20; don't rely on retrospection to convince yourself that these tools of action are essential to your success, by then too many battles will have been lost.

As you live and grow, the strategy of the Mind Accelerator remains an integral component of your existence if you want to live in an accelerated capacity. Look at the side of the pages of this book and you will notice four distinct regions where a black bleed appears at the edge of the page. These four sections of the book are where the four systems of action that should be used on a continuous basis are located. These strategies represent the four-cylinder power plant of a successful existence. Adopt these four strategies and you will live a life all others will envy.

"In the arena of human life the honours and rewards fall to those who show their good qualities in action."

Aristotle

"The beginning of a habit is like an invisible thread, but every time we repeat the act we strengthen the strand, add to it another filament, until it becomes a great cable and binds us irrevocably, in thought and act."

Orison Swett Marden

Key Success Strategy 1
USE MIND CONDITIONING TO FOCUS YOUR THOUGHTS AND REFINE YOUR SELF-CONCEPT EVERY MORNING AND JUST BEFORE BED

Key Success Strategy 2
USE THE INFINITY MIND SYSTEM AND INCREASE YOUR IQ WITH 15 MINUTES OF USE EACH DAY

Key Success Strategy 3
USE THE INFINITY READING SYSTEM TO IREAD ONE BOOK OR INFORMATION SOURCE EACH DAY

Key Success Strategy 4
USE GOAL CHARGING TO PROGRAM OBJECTIVES INTO YOUR SUBCONSCIOUS EVERY MORNING

Those who rely on ability and aptitude rarely prove to be great contenders, but those who rely on stratagem and wisdom—those skilled tacticians who compete with weapons that have proven their worth and tools that have shown their potency, will always prove unassailable. Those armed with the stratagem contained herein don't rely on meeting with easily-defeated opponents or weak competition for their victory. They don't depend on luck and easy breaks. They rely on themselves, for no matter what the obstacle, they are armed for triumph. No matter the width of the chasm or the height of the mountain, they will conquer all by competing with tactical force and by cunningly outsmarting their opponent. The external world is full of unknown factors and unpredictable events. Rely on yourself. Rely on your *proven* ability to succeed and you will never face a challenge too great.

WITH THE MIND ACCELERATOR, YOU HAVE THE STRATEGY AND COURAGE TO CHART A NEW COURSE. MAINTAIN FORWARD PROGRESSION AND BECOME A TRUE CITIZEN OF SUCCESS BY CONTINUING TO PUT THE MA PHENOMENON TO WORK.

iReading Training

Use these four pages to train your eyes to focus on the page in a divergent fashion and practice maintaining the illusionary third page while blinking and turning the page back and forth.

To make it easier for you to override the temptation of hard focusing on the text, the text is reversed; even so, your mind can still absorb the textual information on the page. If you find it helps you develop your iReading skill, you can execute Step One of iReading while holding the book upside down. Your mind instantaneously flips it right side up so your comprehension won't suffer in the slightest.

To visually capture the information on each page, you must undergo an alteration in your point of awareness, and achieve a shift in perspective.

With the book in front of you, try imagining yourself floating just above and behind where you are currently sitting. You are suspended and hovering in full defiance of gravity; your eyes are looking at the book from a vantage point that is just above and slightly behind your head. Envision yourself gazing at the page from just behind yourself - as if you've psychologically stepped out of your physical body, and your metaphysical self is leaning over the top of your physical self, and peering at the page. This perspective will widen your field of sight - allowing you to fully capture both facing pages—the entire reading surface with one glance.

As you fixedly gaze at the centre crease of the book, not only can you see the 4 corners of the book, but you can also see the things surrounding you by using your peripheral vision. Notice the room around you, not by shifting you eyes, but by maintaining steady focus on the centre crease and using your peripheral vision. See the walls surrounding you, the floor beneath you, and the ceiling above you. Try to keep your field of sight open and again, notice the 4 corners of the book in your periph- eral vision; see the full 2 pages, detect the 4 corners, and steadily gaze at the centre crease. There should be a distinct clarity and focus to the book.

Now try to visualize an X connecting these 4 corners, with your gaze directed at the centre of this X. While looking at the centre of this X, soften your gaze and notice the white space surrounding the letters, the white space surrounding the paragraphs, and the pattern that the white space forms between the paragraphs. Maintain a strong awareness of the white space and the 4 corners, while simply noticing the text. Maintain a soft gaze on these features of book, never hard focusing in on the text

The major intention of this step is to achieve divergent eyes. What are divergent eyes? When one normally reads a book, there eyes converge on each word and sentence—hard focusing. When looking at your nose you are converging your eyes to the maximum extent, as each eye points inward. When your eyes come together, they are converging.

Diverging your eyes means to split them apart, so to do so to the maximum extent, would perhaps be to look at the moon, or a far off star. To achieve divergent eyes, you must do the exact opposite—make your eyes look forward in a broader capacity. With the book in your hands and in front of you, fix your gaze on a spot on the wall, beyond the top of the book. Your eyes are peering outward, and your peripheral vision is allowing you to be fully aware of what is going on around you.

Now slowly bring the book in your line of sight, and as you do so, try to maintain your divergent focus on what is beyond the book. Imagine you have x-ray vision, and can see clear through the centre crease. Beam your eyes right through the centre of the book at your focal plane beyond the centre crease as if you have laser sight. This will cause the plane of the book to look blurry, and fuzzy. Keep this relaxed divergent gaze, and maintain this softer focus on the book.

Bring your attention to the blurriness that this divergent gaze creates around the centre crease, and you will notice that there appears to be two centre creases, and between these two illusionary creases, a third page. Seeing this third page is a tell tale sign that you have correctly shifted your perspective, and have achieved divergent eyes.

At first, it will be difficult to do maintain this third middle page. When you look beyond the book, and slowly bring the book into your plan of sight, you may lose the third page quite easily. At first, move just the tip of the book in your line of gaze to see the third page. You should be able to easily see it, but maintaining it takes some training. Practice keeping that third page in sight by slowly moving the book in and out of position, moving just the top of the book in and out of your line of sight. Practice closing your eyes for a few seconds, and maintaing the illusionary third page. Try rapidly blinking while keeping the third page in sight. By trying different things, and putting in the necessary time, you will quickly become proficient at shifting your ocular focus. To train your eyes, refer to the section at the back of the book called iReading Training.

Once you can see the illusionary third page that your eyes create, and maintain its presence, you'll know that you have achieved the soft focus needed for iReading—and you'll have properly executed the first major step to unbounded information capture.

As a human being raised in our modern culture, you have surely been taught to closely follow each word and sentence with strict concentration as you read, since birth. As children, many of us used our finger to follow along, and many of us formed the habit of mouthing each word, or even reading aloud. It is our natural inclination to hard focus on each word and sentence. Going against this, as trained within this book is like going against a lifetime of customary convention and habit. Developing the ability to soft focus on a page, and maintain such a focus for the remainder of a book takes practice. The temptation to focus in on words and sentences is strong at first, so you must train yourself to resist this tendency.

Realize this, and resolve to gain the ability to attain a soft focus. You have the ability, it is just a matter of rewiring your eyes- by going against your natural instincts, and practicing until it becomes second nature.

Using your eyes differently and maintaining your alpha mind state as and directly enter your subconscious. By keeping your eyes from form-ing a definite and hard focus, and directing your gaze at the centre of the page, you can engage your subconscious and capture the whole page of text.

For the first several books you iRead, an entire 300 page book will take you 10 minutes, while a 600 page book will take 20 minutes. As you become more advanced, begin to turn the pages more quickly, and spend as little as 1 second on each page. Advanced iReaders can work through a 600 page book in 10 minutes.

To maintain an achievement oriented focus throughout the entire book, advance through the material with a steady mantra, and in a rhythmic manner. With your breathing deep and even, and your chant steady and rhythmic, you will maintain the alpha state of mind, keep your subconscious engaged, and fully capture the text.

As you progress through the book, keep your conscious mind free of negative thoughts, and attention grabbers by gently deflecting them away, and keeping your mind monopolized and focused on your rhyth-mic chant.

Distractions and self destructive thoughts can deter your focus, and sabotage your performance. It is important to keep them at bay by catching them quickly, and ridding them from your mind. Keep yourself from hard focusing in on the text. Preserve your soft focus, sensing the 4 corners of the page and your fingers holding the book, see-ing the illusionary 3rd page, maintaining a strong awareness of the white space around the text, all the while keeping your eyes directed at the centre crease.

You've finished reading the book, but before you activate the informa-tion, you must give the material time to incubate, and simmer within the recesses of your mind. The information in the page and your fingers

volition thought house

a vision realized

"WE ARE AN ORGANIZATION UNITED TOWARDS ONE GOAL: TO INSPIRE CHANGE BY SHOWERING THE AGENTS OF CHANGE UPON THE POPULACE AND LEVERAGING THE COLLECTIVE VOLITION OF EVERY LAST MIND UNTIL THE ROOTS OF OUR PAST ARE LIFTED AND THE ROOTS OF OUR FUTURE CAN TAKE HOLD."

Taylor Wilson, author of *The Mind Accelerator* and founder of Volition Thought House

Forged upon a framework of revolutionary vision, Volition Thought House is an organization dedicated to change all that revolves around it: people, organizations, educational systems, government and the further. The future holds profound change, but at VTH it's an organizational belief that change can be realized only with purposeful action; evolutionary change must be sparked one thought at a time, one act upon another.

Through intuitive research and inventive insight, our team creates change-inducing solutions: educational media engineered to pervade the social consciousness, alter the brand of dominant thought, create success for those who encounter it, and elevate our status as a species—one mind at a time.

Dreams are an integral part of the human condition, the ethereal engine behind the improvement and advancement of the human species. The more that share one of the same dream the greater the odds are that the dream becomes tangible, concrete— that it becomes reality. partnerMIND is an all-encompassing partner structure intended to bring together those with one common dream and aspiration: greater access to the human mind.

Without dreams this partnership platform would be inconceivable. partnerMIND derives its power from the dreams, ideas, imagination and motivation from all those who like Volition Thought House itself, believe in and embody such dreams. As a standalone entity partnerMIND is nothing more than the dream of one, but unite those dreamers that exemplify the ideals and vision behind partnerMIND and it becomes the dream of many. What can such a collection of dreamers accomplish?

A lot. A lot more than exponential upward fluxes in innovation, profits or GDP. They are in the position to usher in a new age—the era of the limitless mind. Unlocking the enormous potential that is our heritage will set loose unequalled change throughout our global civilization, outpacing the enlightenment, the renaissance and the industrial age.

We're on the on the cusp of a new time in human history that will forever change the possibilities and opportunities our nations face. Generations have lived and died, but finally, every man and woman's thoughts and dreams are ours to realize.

To learn more about partnerMIND and the opportunity it represents for corporate organizations, education boards, government and those who dream big, go to **www.partnerMIND.info** .